The Troller's Handbook

Ray Rychnovsky

About the Author

Ray has gone on family fishing trips since he was six years old. He is a fly fisherman, bass fisherman and ocean fisherman and has caught almost every fresh and saltwater fish in the Midwest and Western United States, Canada, Alaska and Mexico. He has found trolling is the most effective and versatile method to find and catch fish.

Ray has had more than 340 feature articles published in national and regional magazines and is the San Francisco Bay Area columnist for *Fishing & Hunting News*. His photos have been recognized with many national, state and regional awards including two first place awards in the color scenic photo contests of the Outdoor Writers Association of America. His articles have received awards at the state level. He is president of the Outdoor Writers Association of California and an active member of the Outdoor Writers Association of America.

Rychnovsky graduated at the top of his class when he earned a Master of Science degree in engineering mechanics and taught that subject in college. He has worked in aerodynamics and has been awarded two patents including one for a lifting parachute. When he was studying partial differential equations in college, he developed and solved the equations to evaluate the line profile through the water and the depth a bait or lure is trolled for various weights, speeds and line sizes. He has written extensively about trolling including an article in *Outdoor Life* in 1985 showing conclusions from his trolling depth study. He developed and solved equations for trolling with a downrigger and published the results in *Salt Water Sportsman* in 1990.

All inquiries should be addressed to:
Frank Amato Publications, Inc.
P.O. Box 82112 • Portland, Oregon 97282 • 503-653-8108

Book Design: Amy Tomlinson
Photography and Graphs: Ray Rychnovsky
Diagram pg. 88: Ray Rychnovsky
Diagram, pg. 47, photo pg. 85 from *Black Box Electric Fishing Technology*
by Malcolm Russell and Dick Pool
Luhr-Speed photo on pg. 73 courtesy of Luhr-Jensen.

Printed in Canada
1 3 5 7 9 10 8 6 4 2

ISBN: 1-57188-122-0   UPC: 0-66066-00320-1

TABLE OF

Contents

Foreword

I had the opportunity to observe an FB111 training exercise in a flight simulator at Plattsburg Air Force base in New York. The pilot and weapons officer had years of training and experience and I expected them to solve every problem instantly. But that isn't what happened. Oh yes, when they got a "missile fired" warning, they ejected flares and the pilot made evasive maneuvers with the quickness of a cat. But, for other problems like an engine warning, they reached for their manuals. They had manuals under their seats, between their seats and in overhead compartments and before the training mission was over, they used every one of those manuals. They probably spent more time consulting manuals than actively flying the airplane.

This book starts with basics for trolling and covers simple to advanced methods. It describes how to troll for many freshwater and saltwater species. Tackle, boat and electronics that will help you be a more successful angler are described. Anglers who use this book will apply basic science to get their lure or bait to the proper depth and learn trolling methods to catch more fish.

The heart of this book is the graphs in Chapters 9, 10 and 11. These are the first complete set of graphs ever published showing how to troll at a desired depth. Graphs in these chapters show how to get your lure or bait to the fish's depth for all normal freshwater and saltwater trolling. Just as the crew of the FB111 didn't immediately know how to solve every problem, you aren't going to know exactly how to set up for trolling for every depth and every circumstance. But this book is intended to be used as the pilot's manual. Take this handbook in your boat and when you find fish at a given depth, pull it out, turn to the graph that applies and set up to troll that depth.

Easy-to-use graphs pinpoint your trolled depth with a lure or with a lure behind a weight, with downriggers, and with lead-core or steel line. Sections for different line weights and different trolling conditions cover all of the commonly trolled scenarios and some that aren't so common. You will know the profile of the line, and the depth of the weight or lure as it slices through the water. And you will see the same results for trolling with lead-core line, steel line or downriggers. You will learn what parameters are most important and which ones you can ignore. This turns *guessing* how to get to the proper depth into *knowing* how to troll at the proper depth.

If you are new to trolling or are a novice angler, the first chapters give basics of trolling so you can get started and catch fish. If you just want to know how deep you are trolling, go directly to the graphs in Chapters 9 through 11. For more advanced trolling, including a description of the electronic black box that attracts fish, refer to Chapters 12 through 15. If you are mathematically inclined and want to understand the details of the analysis, read the appendix.

Apply the graphs and principles in this book and you will be a more successful angler.

Anglers drift-fish for striped bass off the Golden Gate Bridge. Drift-fishing is a form of slow trolling.

CHAPTER 1

Trolling

Problems and Solutions

Trolling is the number one fish-catching method for anglers fishing from a boat. More fish are caught trolling than by any other method, except possibly bait-fishing. Trolling gives a lure or bait the natural action that entices a fish to strike. It is a basic fishing method to search for and catch fish—many kinds of fish in many different situations.

When fish are scattered, trolling covers a lot of water to find them. When salmon in rivers are reluctant biters, back-trolling entices them to bite. When looking for tuna or wahoo in the open ocean, high speed trolling finds and catches these fish. For salmon in the ocean or trout in lakes, trolling is a very versatile and effective fishing method. Learn to troll and you can catch almost all species of game fish in rivers, lakes and the ocean under most conditions.

Sometimes trolling is the method used to find and catch fish. At other times, as when fishing for tuna, trolling is the method to locate a school of fish. Once located, the preferred fishing method may be to drift or fish from anchor to catch as many fish as possible from the school. But unless you find that school, you won't catch fish and trolling is the key to finding them.

Trolling is an easy fishing method to learn and apply. It doesn't take accurate casts; it doesn't take special equipment. Basic fishing tackle and basic fishing skills will suffice. Trollers can use inexpensive boats or rent boats at most lakes. An angler fishing from a float tube can even troll by slowly swimming backwards and trolling a fly or lure.

One shortcoming of trolling is that anglers have not known how deep they are trolling. Graphs in this book solve this problem so anglers can get their lure or bait to the fish they see on their fish finder.

Trolling Catches Most Species

Almost every species can be caught trolling—trout, walleye, northern pike, bass, salmon, mackinaw, tuna, yellowtail, wahoo, striped bass, halibut, crappie and many other species are caught trolling. Even bottom-dwelling catfish in freshwater and lingcod and rockfish in the ocean are occasionally caught trolling.

If you have any doubts about how effective trolling is, consider that commercial salmon fishermen who must catch fish for a living select trolling as their best fishing method.

On a trip to the Kvichak River in Alaska a few years ago I had a vivid illustration of how effective trolling can be. I wanted to catch a 10-pound wild trout on a fly rod. The Kvichak is the outlet of Lake Illiamna, the largest lake in Alaska, and the trout grow very large. Catching a 10-pound trout there in late fall when I was fishing wasn't too much to expect when fish were in the river, but this year trout were late moving from the lake to the river. After three days of fishing, I had caught a few pink salmon and only a couple of small trout—far smaller than the 10-pound fish I sought. Anglers who trolled at the same time averaged one to three large trout a day.

My last morning I decided to abandon my dream of a 10-pound wild trout on a fly rod; I wanted the most effective fishing method and that was trolling.

I trolled for five hours and caught and released nine trout each weighing eight to 13 pounds. Trolling can be a very effective fishing method.

Trolling is Very Versatile

Some form of trolling will catch fish under almost any condition. Skip your bait or lure along the surface at high speed for tuna. If fish are shallow, troll with a

lure or flashers on monofilament line; if they are mid-depth, troll with lead-core line or add weight or a diving plane to take your bait or lure to their depth, or use downriggers. If fish are very deep use downriggers or troll with wire

Anglers troll for silver salmon out of Rivers Inlet in British Columbia.

line to get down to them. Troll bait, spoons or crankbaits alone or augmented with attractors like flashers or dodgers.

Trolling is very effective for three reasons. First, trolling is fishing continuously. The lure or bait is always working at an ideal depth—not like casting and retrieving when the lure is at the proper depth a small part of the time. Secondly, it presents the bait or lure in a very natural way—it looks like a vulnerable food fish swimming along just waiting to be eaten. Lastly, trolling covers a lot of territory searching for fish. Bait fishing waits for the fish to come to you. If you can pinpoint where fish are located, bait-fishing or casting and retrieving lures is effective but if you need to search out fish, trolling is a much better fishing method.

Other Forms of Trolling

Usually when I talk of trolling, I mean conventional trolling, motoring through the water, using lures or bait to entice fish. But any time you are moving through the water, you are trolling and these results apply.

If you say, "I don't troll for salmon; I drift-mooch for them," this book still applies. Drift-mooching is a form of trolling at a slow speed. The wind is pushing your boat along; you are moving relative to the water and that is trolling.

When you are drift-mooching for salmon at a depth of 30 feet, and the wind is moving the boat along at perhaps a half knot, you know you only need to pull out 30 feet of line to get to the salmon's depth. But when the wind is moving your boat at a brisk speed and you want to catch salmon 200 feet deep, you need the results of this study to see how deep you are fishing. You also want to know if your line is crossing the line of the angler fishing from the other side of the boat. Graphs in Chapter 10 will help answer these questions.

Your first challenge is to find the appropriate trolling location. Working off points and into coves is a good starting procedure for freshwater fish in lakes. Fishing deep holes where trout hold or where migrating salmon and steelhead rest is the right place to start fishing in rivers. The first few chapters of this book describe the basics of trolling for several species. This section will help you find fish, detect how deep the fish are and learn how to troll to catch them.

A brown pelican flies around the boat.

My final reason for trolling has nothing to do with catching fish. The pace is slow and you have time to drink in the beauty of the surroundings and nearby animals. You are continuously moving, seeing new scenes, maybe coming upon a deer drinking at the shore or an eagle or osprey flying overhead or semi-tame ducks following along saying, "Feed me," as distinctly as if they could talk. By using a quiet electric trolling motor, you can hear the sounds of birds and animals, and your time on the water is relaxing and therapeutic.

Trolling Finds Fish

If fish are scattered, troll to search and find them. Then decide if continuing to troll is the best fishing method. When fishing for tuna or wahoo, trolling is usually the way to find a school of fish. After that, you may drift and cast live bait or lures to get instant hook-ups.

Usually trolling is the method to catch trout but sometimes it can be a locator method for this species. I trolled for trout at a local lake with Stewart Griffiths. We trolled past one point and both of us caught a fish, made a circle, and got another double hook-up on our second pass. We decided we had located a school of hungry trout so we stopped and fly fished. The fish continued to bite and we got to catch them on flies. Even when fish are schooled and you can use bait or cast lures, trolling's natural presentation may be the best way to

Humpback whales feed on herring by herding them to the surface then come out of the water as they chase the herring to the surface.

catch them. Circling back through the school of fish will often catch many fish from that school, sometimes several at a time.

With GPS and sophisticated fish finders to help find fish, downriggers to put your lure in front of fish and black box electronics to attract them, trolling becomes an even more effective fishing method.

Common Misconceptions About Trolling

The depth fished when trolling at an intermediate depth has been a mystery. When the line disappears into the water, all knowledge of the depth of the lure or bait seems to disappear as well.

One book showed line going steeply into the water then becoming horizontal at the weight. The opposite is true—it is more vertical near the weight or lure becoming more horizontal at the surface of the water. With a light lure or weight, or a shallow running lure, the line may be almost horizontal for its entire length with the lure trolled very shallow.

One way to visualize the contour of the line when you are trolling is to drop the weight or lure into the water, stop for a moment when the lure or weight is a couple of feet deep and see what angle the line makes coming out of the water. That is the angle of the line under the water. Let out a few more feet of line and note the line makes a more shallow angle. The angle of each segment of line under the water doesn't change as you let more line out and the line goes deeper. It can be just under the surface or several hundred feet deep and the angle and contour of that segment of line doesn't change.

Think of a series of short segments of line, one connected to the next, to visualize the line under water. With a moderate weight, the line at the weight is almost vertical when it is just under the surface of the water and it is still almost vertical after you let out 100 feet of line. If the angle of a segment of line ten feet from the lure or weight is 65 degrees as that segment enters the water, the angle of that particular segment of line when trolled at the same velocity is still 65 degrees when it is 10 feet, 100 feet or 1000 feet deep.

Some anglers have told me a lure becomes more shallow as you let more line out. That isn't true. As you put out more line, the angle of the line as it enters the water becomes more and more shallow until the line eventually rides on top of the water, and the lure doesn't go any deeper. After you let out 50 to 100 feet of line with light weights, the lure will be near its maximum depth—you can let out several hundred more feet of line and the lure or bait doesn't go deeper but it doesn't get shallower.

One guide and lecturer who obviously doesn't know hydrodynamics said a light lure fished from a monofilament line would troll near the surface of the water. He then said when he put the line on his downrigger and lowered the downrigger 10 feet deep, his lure was seven feet under the surface. Not true—the lure is actually slightly deeper than 10 feet—nothing is lifting that lure, gravity is actually pulling it down slightly.

One manufacturer of downriggers calculated how deep the downrigger weight and thus the lure was running by taking the angle the downrigger cable entered the water and the length of line, then projecting that line straight into the water. He used trigonometry to calculate the depth of the downrigger weight. The bow in the line does lift the weight so it isn't as deep as indicated on the downrigger counter. But he overcompensated projecting his weight to be more shallow than it really was and his error was often larger than just believing the depth on his indicator.

Getting to the Right Depth

Anglers fishing moderately deep at normal trolling speed can use downriggers to get their lure accurately to the desired depth but most anglers don't have downriggers. Even if they do, downriggers can be cumbersome and anglers may leave them home or not use them. Anglers can use lead-core line and have a better idea of how deep they are trolling. But most of the time they are trolling with monofilament line and using the weight of the lure or adding weights to get to depth.

You see fish on your fish finder and know how deep you should be trolling but how do you get your trolled bait or lure to the right depth? You can guess how deep you are trolling but your guess may not be even close. The graphs in this book show you how to fish the desired depth.

The physical principles that control trolled depth are known, the contour of the line in the water and the depth of the weight or lure can be calculated. I have made these calculations for most fishing conditions. The graphs in Chapters 9, 10 and 11 show how deep you are trolling. You can use them to choose a weight and line length to troll the right depth. You will know how deep you are trolling and how to get your lure to the fish showing up on your fish finder.

These graphs give accurate depths for trolling with a line and weight or lure, for a downrigger and for lead-core and steel line for a wide range of trolling velocities, line diameters and weights. Troll with two-pound to 100-pound-test line and a fraction of an ounce to a couple pounds of weight and one of the graphs will apply. Troll with lead-core or steel line or with downriggers and other graphs will show you how to get to the desired depth.

The first requirement to catch fish trolling is to get your bait or lure to the fish's depth. The graphs in this book will show you how to do that.

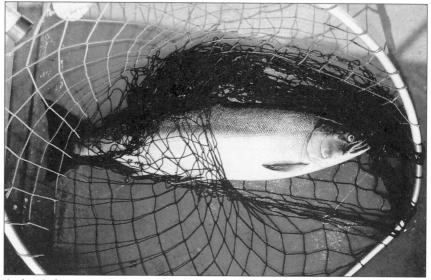

A salmon in the net.

CHAPTER 2

Trolling for Trout in Lakes

Traditional trout fishing in streams and rivers is fly fishing, casting lures or fishing with bait. In lakes that turns to trolling or bait-fishing. Trolling for trout only a few years ago was at large lakes—often very large lakes away from population centers. Lakes such as Pend Oreille Lake in northern Idaho, Lake Tahoe, Flathead Lake in Montana, Flaming Gorge and many others have wild trout. Trolling is one of the best ways to catch these trout.

This has all changed with the advent of large trout stocking programs for urban lakes. Today most trolling for trout takes place in lakes near cities and towns and the catch is planted trout. Trout are stocked in almost every lake that has water cool enough to hold them—particularly in lakes in and near populated areas where the demand for fishing recreation is high but water resources are limited. Anglers pay a fishing fee to cover the cost—typically about $3 per day at public lakes. Bait-fishing and trolling are about equally popular ways to catch these fish.

A typical trout-fishing trip for wild trout may take several days, but anglers can travel to urban lakes in a morning or evening, catch fish and return home. The appeal of catching a wild trout has been replaced by the chance to catch large hatchery-grown trout—sometimes very large trout. Anglers occasionally land trout exceeding 10 pounds; some weigh 15 pounds or more.

Urban lakes are planted with trout from a private hatchery.

These fish are strong and challenging but not usually acrobatic. However, when a lake has just reopened to fishing or when lakes cool and fish come to the surface, carryover trout from the previous year have grown into almost wild fish that may jump and fight extra hard.

Whether you are fishing for wild trout in remote lakes or planters in urban lakes, the most basic fishing method is to troll with a small lure like a Kastmaster, Z-Ray, Needlefish, Triple Teazer or a crankbait like a Rapala or Rat-L-Trap to imitate small baitfish in the lake. You can troll lures or bait with or without flashers near the surface on small diameter lines, troll them off downriggers, use lead-core line or weights or diving planes to fish deep.

Trolling with Monofilament Line

When fish are shallow many anglers troll with monofilament line using a light lure or a night crawler behind flashers. The attractor isn't very deep but it is very gaudy; fish can't miss it, rise to the flasher and take the bait or lure behind the attractor. Flashers are made to represent a school of swimming baitfish, but whether this is the reason or they just reflect a lot of light to get attention, they work.

Fishing with flashers is a perfectly good way to catch these

John Caulfield shows off a large trout being tagged for an urban lake.

trout but I don't use them. They add a resistance when fighting the fish. When the fish swims laterally, the flasher is pulling against the water creating an extra unwanted force. I don't have a good feel for what the fish is doing or the confidence that I can always react to fight the fish in the best way. When I have tried flashers, a friend trolling with a small lure usually caught more fish. When fish are biting, I have been able to troll at the appropriate depth and catch them on small lures without flashers.

The flashers must be trolled slowly—slower than idle speed on most outboard motors. A trolling plate to block some of the flow from the propeller or an electric trolling motor may be required to slow the boat to the ideal, slow trolling speed.

Get the Lure to the Fish's Depth

Lures like Kastmaster, Z-Ray or Cripplure are heavier lures that get down a few feet below the surface. They can be trolled at a good depth from fall to spring when fish are shallow. When fish are deeper or when trolling with lighter lures, add weight to get the lure deeper. The graphs in Chapters 10 and 11 show how much weight to add to get to the desired depth.

When you use a weight to take your lure to depth, light lures like Needlefish, Triple Teazers, Dick Nites or Humdingers are ideal. They don't add much drag to the weight and don't tend to dive down because of their own weight. They just follow along behind the weight. Get the weight to the right depth and you have the lure at the right depth.

Troll the lure a long distance behind the boat so the boat passes over the fish and they have time to disassociate the lure from the boat. Fifty feet of trail (the horizontal distance from the boat to the lure) may be fine in murky water or when fish are deep, but 75 to 100 feet of trail will often catch more fish in clear water.

Fly Anglers Troll Flies

I fly fished with famous fly fishing guide J. Fair on Davis Lake in California last spring. We started early in the morning, climbed in his boat and motored across the lake where Fair expected to find fish. We beached the boat, got out and started fishing. Using an olive Woolly Bugger that Fair tied, I waded out along a shallow point and started casting in areas where Fair had caught trout the previous morning. Occasionally I would see a trout rise and I would try to cast to that fish, however most of the time I didn't see any rising fish but cast hoping to entice a cruising fish.

After an hour without a fish we moved to another area and did the same thing for another hour. I was surprised when Fair, one of the best fly fishing anglers I know, switched to trolling. If he wasn't acting as a guide, he might fish all day using traditional fly fishing. But as a guide, he needed to get fish for his clients and he needed to have a full bag of tricks when one fishing method wasn't working. He knows trolling can be one of the most effective fish catching methods.

We changed to bait-casting rods and tied on Woolly Bugger flies. The conventional revolving spool reel had a 15-foot length of lead-core line to sink the fly followed by monofilament running line and we let our flies out about 100 feet behind the boat.

By the end of the day, two companions and I caught four fish using traditional fly fishing but we landed nine trout trolling.

Catch Large Fish

Many anglers are very successful trollers catching hundreds of trout in a season but most of them are small- to medium-sized fish. Others don't catch as many fish but catch large trout. Niel Nielsen, retired manager of San Pablo Reservoir, is one of a few people who consistently lands large fish. In three months in the spring of 1996, he caught 18 trout weighing more than five pounds with several in the nine- to 12-pound range.

His first rule in trolling for large fish is, "Slow down; then go slower." He trolls at a speed of 0.9 to 1.0 mph.

Nielsen says trolling requires a lot of patience. "It may take time to find the secret or they may just not be biting. But when you have found the right combination of lure, depth and trolling speed, and fish are biting, you have a good chance to catch several large fish."

He wants his lure well behind the boat. When he is trolling off downriggers, he lets out 45 to 50 feet of line before he attaches his lure to the downrigger. With a lure like a Rapala on monofilament, he trolls about 70 feet behind the boat. He experiments to find where the fish strike and that may not be where they are showing on his fish finder. He says he has set his downrigger to 15 feet even though fish are showing on his fish finder at 20 to 30 feet. Fishing a little above the fish is better than fishing below them.

Nielsen uses a variety of lures but likes Needlefish, particularly the new hot tail design, Dick Nites, Rainbow Raiders and Rapalas. He particularly likes the Pearl Bikini Needlefish and Fire Tiger Rapala and has good success with red and silver, chartreuse or red and white lures. He said a hot lure recently has been a white lure with a green head but the best color combinations change frequently. On clear days he likes silver lures and on overcast days or in murky water he favors gold lures.

Nielsen believes scent is an important factor and tries to avoid negative scents. He doesn't routinely use scent but sometimes applies them to his lures to mask scents they may have picked up from his hands.

If you want to catch more large fish, try Nielsen's fishing techniques.

Turn Over Trout

With the arrival of fall, the days grow short and a chill fills the air. Lakes cool and trout fishing takes an abrupt change. Fish that were deep swim to the surface. Large, fat trout are now easy targets for anglers.

What triggers this change? To answer this question, let's start in the spring when trout are driven deep. As spring and summer days grow longer and warmer, the warm air and radiation from the sun warms the surface layer of water in lakes. Warm water rises to the top of the lake so this warm water stays on the surface. Wind and waves mix the water but only to a certain depth and the cool water remains at the bottom. The lake becomes stratified with a layer of oxygen-rich warm water on the surface, a layer of cool oxygen-depleted water in the bottom and a seam where these two meet called the thermocline.

Peter Liebold holds a troll-caught trout.

The temperature change at the thermocline is abrupt. I have dropped a temperature sensor connected to an electrical readout in the boat. As the probe goes deeper and deeper, the temperature stays the same but when it comes to this layer, the temperature drops five or ten degrees.

This narrow zone, the thermocline, is the only depth that has everything trout and baitfish demand. It has cool waters, food and oxygen and this is where trout thrive during the warmer months. Troll at that depth or a little shallower and you will be at the right depth to catch them.

In the fall the surface of the lake cools but cold water falls as warm water rises. This action mixes the water from the surface to the depths of the lake. The cool, oxygenated water near the surface is ideal for trout and for baitfish. Trout now move to the surface to find the desired water temperature, oxygen and food.

A special time to fish in urban lakes is when trout first come to the surface. These fish have lived deep in the lake during the summer and have become acclimated to their environment. They fight more like wild trout than hatchery plants. Supplemented by weekly plants, good fishing continues throughout the fall, winter and into spring.

Another special time to catch trout is when lakes reopen after being closed. San Pablo Reservoir in the San Francisco Bay Area and Lake Pardee in the foothills east of Stockton are waterfowl refuges and are closed to fishing from mid-November to mid-February. Many carryover trout have grown almost wild and are great fighters yet they are eager to take a bait. Later they will become educated and wary of a bait or lure.

14

During these cooler months, trout are seen surfacing frequently but they may be holding five to 15 feet deep and this is the place to start fishing. Fish this depth in the early morning and go deeper as the sun drives fish down. Shallow-running crankbaits or medium-weight lures trolled on monofilament line with no weight or a light weight will get the lure to the desired depth. A light lure trolled on 30 to 60 feet of lead-core line will also get the lure to the proper depth.

Catching Reluctant Fish

Often you see fish on your depth finder and know your lure is at the right depth but the fish aren't hitting. For some reason, fish seem to have periods of feeding when they hit almost any lure or bait and other times when they are very finicky. Being able to entice them to strike when they are not actively feeding makes the day. At these times, special maneuvers may put extra fish in the boat.

Sometimes trout hit when your boat is making a turn. As you turn, the lure takes a shorter curve inside the path of the boat. It goes slower, drops deeper, then speeds back to normal trolling speed and climbs back to the normal trolling depth. The change in depth exposes the lure to deeper fish, the increase in speed and climbing may give the illusion of a meal getting away and trigger a strike.

I fished with one guide who trolled a downrigger 40 feet deep and we could see the downrigger weight on his fish finder. Once we could also see a trout coming up from under and behind the weight following the lure. The fish followed along without attacking until we changed velocity. We sped up; the fish reacted, took the lure and we had a fish. It probably

This trout was caught on a small lure trolled off lead-core line.

thought the potential meal was getting away when we increased the lure's speed and the trout decided it had to act or its dinner would escape.

Tricks for Trolling

J. Fair had us hold our rod tips to the side of the boat at Davis Lake and slowly rotate the tips in about a 10-inch diameter circle as we trolled. Rather than the fly traveling through the water at a constant speed, it would speed up then slow down as we moved our rod tip. At other times I have swept the rod tip forward then back but Fair has found this motion to be too abrupt and jerky when trolling flies. Rotating the rod tip gives a smoother, more natural and more effective action. When trolling a crankbait or small lure, the more abrupt change may be better.

Frequently, when you increase velocity, as when you start reeling in your lure, a fish hits. One guide had me pump my rod tip as I retrieved my lure. This action increased the speed of the lure, then slowed it down to make it look alive. Another guide I fished with frequently increased the speed of the motor momentarily then dropped back to normal trolling speed. Changing speed and changing depths often draws strikes.

Tackle and Boat

Basic fishing tackle is all that is needed to troll for trout. A 6 1/2- or 7-foot-long lightweight rod with a spinning reel or a conventional bait casting reel is ideal. For urban lakes, light line is required and that means six-pound or perhaps four-pound-test monofilament line. With the new high strength super lines like Fireline or Spiderwire, the line can be a bit stronger and still have the desired small diameter. I have had success tying the lure directly to Fireline but am concerned about visibility of some of the other lines. A clear leader may make sense with those lines.

My favorite light trout lures include Dick Nites, Triple Teazers, Needlefish, Lucky Knights and Canadian Wonders. For heavier lures I like Kastmasters, Cripplures and Z-Rays. You can fish these without extra weight or add weight to get them very deep. Crankbaits are often very good trolling lures. Rapalas, Rebels, Rat-L-Traps and Wiggle Warts are some of my favorites. Choose sizes to imitate the bait in a lake. For lakes with minnows and threadfin shad, lures should be small.

Lead-core line is a good way to get to fish from a few feet under the surface in the normal cool weather pattern to deep fish in the thermocline in the summer. Fishing with this line is discussed in Chapter 7.

The primary consideration for a boat is safety. The boat must be large enough to be seaworthy and safe even when unexpected weather blows in. For most moderate or small lakes, a 14- or 15-foot aluminum fishing boat with a 15 horsepower outboard motor is ideal. Set it up with a fish finder, rod holders, a cooler and tackle box along with the appropriate life jackets and other safety gear and you have covered the basics. Add an electric trolling motor (some lakes only permit electric motors) and you are ready to troll at any speed. A smaller boat like a folding or inflatable boat for easy storage, or a variety of small basic boats with electric trolling motors are fine for small urban lakes.

Planting trout in urban lakes has greatly increased fishing opportunity for city and suburban anglers. Whether you're fishing for planted trout near population centers or wild trout in remote lakes, trolling is one of the most effective fishing methods.

CHAPTER 3

Catch Salmon in Saltwater

Trolling for salmon in saltwater takes many different forms. The standard method of trolling from a party boat off the California coast is with a heavy three-pound weight on a sinker release. When a fish strikes, the weight drops free and the fish is played without a weight.

The heavy weight is a struggle to handle and it requires heavy tackle—far heavier than is needed to play the fish. Most anglers

The party boat Happy Hooker *drift-mooches for salmon. This is a form of slow trolling.*

object to the heavy weight and stout tackle but fishing with them gives anglers two advantages. Heavy weights take the bait or lure almost straight down to a known depth and allows many anglers to fish close together on a boat.

Drift-mooching Preferred
Fishing in saltwater for salmon off the California coast has made a dramatic transition in fishing methods in the last few years. Until 15 years ago, trolling with heavy weights was virtually the only way party boat anglers in California fished for salmon. Now most anglers on party boats drift-mooch to catch their salmon. A light weight is used for mooching; a much lighter, more limber rod can now be used and playing the salmon is much more sporting. Mooching seems to be more productive with a lot of bait in the water—such as from a party boat with 15 to 20 anglers on board.

"Early in the season, anchovies and other bait fish have not arrived off the Northern California coast," said Steve Bales, skipper of the *New Fisherman III* out of Berkeley who trolls early in the season then switches to mooching. "Salmon are feeding on krill (a small shrimp) and a baitfish must be well-presented to interest them. They are more attracted to a trolled anchovy that looks like a naturally swimming bait than a drifting bait."

Anglers don't always choose the most successful fishing method. Many anglers only fish from party boats that mooch for salmon. Even when trolling is more successful, they choose party boats that drift-mooch so they can play the fish on light, sporting tackle.

Drift-mooching is a form of trolling. The power is the wind and the speed is slow but you are moving through the water and the contour your line makes in the water may be important.

Advantages of Trolling

After a storm scatters the bait or when salmon are sparse or schools haven't been located, trolling will cover a lot of area and is the best method to locate them. When schools of bait are attracting salmon, you know just where to find the salmon. Mooching is a great fishing method but trolling around the edges of the school of bait is also effective.

Like most people, I prefer mooching with light tackle when fishing from a party boat, but trolling from a small boat is different. Traditional trolling with lighter weights and a couple of downriggers is still an excellent way for anglers to fish from private boats or smaller six-pack charter boats.

Trollers fishing from a small boat don't need the heavy weights and can use a combination of downriggers and rods with lighter weights and light tackle. Four-, six-, eight-ounce and one-pound weights will suffice for trolling when only a few anglers are fishing. You can use light weights on your aft lines and heavier weights on forward lines to separate lines and avoid tangles.

One other advantage of trolling is that a boat moving under power rocks and pitches less and is more comfortable. When drift-mooching, the boat tosses like a cork adrift in rough seas and anglers are more likely to get seasick.

Trolling with a light weight has advantages but the line loops behind the boat and your trolling depth is not obvious. You need to determine your depth and the graphs in Chapter 10 show you how to get to depth with light or moderate weights.

Adapt to Changing Conditions

Reacting to changing conditions helps catch fish. While trolling south of San Francisco with two fishing friends, we had landed only one fish in three hours. As we slowly motored into a new area, the fish finder turned solid black all the

way from 10 to 45 feet down signaling a large school of bait directly under us. Where would the salmon be? Probably right at the bottom of the ball of bait slashing through the school hitting or stunning their prey then circling down below the bait, grabbing the small fish as they fall.

The fish we had seen on our fish finder were shallower so

The skipper on a party boat is ready to net a salmon out of Brookings, Oregon.

our deepest bait was only 30 feet down. Bob Tockey grabbed a rod out of its holder and stripped out about 20 feet of line. The one-pound sinker took the anchovy on a nine-foot leader almost straight down. He dropped the bait down quickly but as it approached its new depth, he slowed the descent to try to simulate an injured fish slowly falling out of the school.

Tockey held the line at his chosen depth for only a moment when a fish hit the bait. He gently lifted the rod; that's all that is required to set the hook. The fish moved sluggishly at first as his lightly set drag played out line to the fish but then it reacted and line came smoking off the spool. The size of a fish can often be gauged by the speed and length of its first run and this one was a good one

18

by that standard. The unmistakable tip-off, however, was the slow pump, pump, pump action as the large fish finned through the water with relatively slow, powerful strokes of its whole body.

About 15 minutes after the fish grabbed the bait I slipped the net in front of the 17-pound salmon and lifted it on board.

In this case getting the bait to the salmon below a school of bait earned a fish. Other times it is changing depth to intercept fish showing up on the fish finder. As the sun comes up, salmon go deeper and changing lures or bait to a deeper depth gets to the fish.

Salmon Species

Five major salmon species are found in the Pacific Ocean off our West Coast. King salmon, also called chinook salmon, are the largest of the salmon species and are found from California to Alaska. Most salmon off California are king salmon and most of the salmon that spawn in California rivers are king salmon. Silver salmon, also known as coho salmon, are the next most important Pacific salmon. Silvers are found from Northern California to the Bering Sea of western Alaska. A few years ago they were the dominant species off Oregon and the northernmost part of California but they are at a low ebb today (many runs of silvers are listed as threatened or endangered) and king salmon dominate the catch in these areas. Silvers are still an abundant and exciting game fish off British Columbia and Alaska and are important to Washington fishing.

The author admires a king salmon.

Chum salmon are the next most important salmon typically weighing about eight to 18 pounds. Sports anglers catch few chums in saltwater. Sockeye and pink salmon are smaller and very abundant. They are important in the commercial catch but are rarely caught in saltwater. Chums, pinks and sockeye are mostly caught by sports anglers in rivers in Alaska and British Columbia and are fun fish on light tackle.

Salmon Range

Salmon range as far south as Los Angeles but only a few salmon are caught in this area during a brief period in the spring. Central California ports of Morro Bay and Avila Beach have good salmon fishing one year and few salmon the next. Monterey and Santa Cruz have reliable salmon fishing and are frequently hot spots in the early spring when salmon season opens. In the San Francisco area, salmon can be caught all season from March to October. Northern California, Oregon and Washington have periods of good salmon catches but the season is very restrictive. Canada and Alaska have great salmon fishing during the summer months when their season is open and anglers come in droves to catch them.

In Alaska, June is the traditional month for king salmon. Almost every river that has these fish has them in June. The inland passages off southeast Alaska and British Columbia have king salmon in June but they also have this species at various times later in the year.

Cohos are found off Alaska from mid-July to September. Some places have an early run in this time period and other areas have late runs. Sockeye, pinks and chums are caught in July and August.

Salmon Conservation

When Lewis and Clark explored the Pacific Northwest, salmon stocks were plentiful. This looked like a resource that would last forever but people underestimated the destruction that could be wrought. With a series of dams on most major rivers, pollution and huge water exportation projects, many runs of salmon in California, Oregon and Washington have been depleted—some are threatened or endangered. The runs that are doing well are mostly fortified by salmon hatcheries that turn out millions of smolt.

To make matters worse, the United States and Canada have squabbled over salmon. Canada says Alaska anglers were catching too many salmon that originated in Canadian waters and are headed back to their home rivers to spawn. Canada retaliated by catching "too many" coho salmon headed toward rivers in Oregon and Washington.

The Columbia River has a series of dams that block salmon from spawning grounds and this has decimated salmon reproduction. Huge water diversions of Northern California water to Central and Southern California spoil the salmon's spawning habitat, and a great many unscreened water diversions take millions of small salmon with the water.

As a result, many of our runs of salmon are threatened, endangered or at critically low levels. Salmon seasons in many places off California, Oregon and Washington are short to almost non-existent and quotas of salmon for both sports anglers and commercial anglers are restrictive. The overall trend is to continuously impose new restrictions to salmon fishing but the news isn't always bad. Occasionally a population of these fish like the Klamath River salmon improves and restrictions are relaxed.

Seasons and regulations change but now most salmon anglers may fish with only one rod. Barbless circle hooks are required along most of California's coast when drift-mooching with bait. Seasons, limits, minimum sizes and regulations change frequently so check the latest restrictions before you start fishing.

Each year you need to evaluate the restrictions and when and where you can fish. When fishing is permitted, it can be very good. For example, the fall run of Sacramento River salmon is doing very well but the winter run is endangered. Restrictions to save the winter run limit catches of the fall run that could sustain higher harvest levels. Don't be put off by the restrictions; many areas still have excellent salmon fishing.

While releasing fish may be laudable, salmon suffer a high release mortality particularly if they are played to exhaustion or are handled during release. Troll-caught salmon are usually easy to release. They are lip hooked; the hook can be removed easily and they have a good chance to survive. Salmon caught with bait mooching are usually deeply hooked and they may or may not survive release.

Fish played to exhaustion have a poor chance of survival when released so fish with tackle sufficiently heavy to quickly land a salmon you may release. Barbless hooks are usually required but even if they aren't, use barbless hooks for easy release. Cut the line without lifting the fish out of the water if you can't easily remove the hook. A salmon may pass the hook through its system or survive with the hook.

Tackle and Fishing Methods

Trolling on a sports fishing boat requires heavy tackle to handle the three-pound trolling weights. A seven-foot rod with a flexible tip but fairly hefty main shaft is

20

ideal. A conventional revolving spool ocean reel with a smooth drag filled with 20- to 25-pound-test line completes the outfit.

A rod for trolling off a downrigger or with a light weight can be much lighter. Anglers sometimes fish with spinning gear but I prefer a

A heavy weight on a sinker release takes the bait or lure to depth when trolling for salmon from a party boat out of California.

conventional revolving spool reel. Sometimes I use a lightweight, seven-foot saltwater rod with an Abu Garcia Ambassador reel filled with 15- or 20-pound-test line. Other times I have used an eight- or nine-foot steelhead rod with a similar reel with 12- to 15-pound-test line.

A good trolling speed is less than two knots. A bait or lure is trolled from a six- to nine-foot leader. When trolling, change to a fresh, quality bait about every 20 minutes; set the bait at the proper depth and be certain the line isn't tangled and the bait is "swimming" naturally. Do all of these well and you have covered the basics to maximize your chances for hooking salmon.

When trolling a heavy weight, pull out one-foot pulls of line to get the desired depth, set the rod in the holder and wait for the fish. If a fish taps the bait but isn't hooked, pull out a couple of eight-inch pulls off the reel to move the bait and try to interest the fish in making a second strike.

The standard bait for trolling is a frozen (and thawed) anchovy rigged on a bait harness hook that is pushed through the length of the fish with its point positioned near the tail of the bait. This hook has two eyes; a pin is pushed from bottom to top of the bait's head securing the hook in position by going through the rear eye of the hook. The hook is clipped to the leader through its forward eye.

Bait on a bait harness hook are good for trolling for salmon.

A Herring Dodger connected to the leader in front of the trolled bait will often entice more strikes. A small size 0/0 is my favorite size dodger. All silver, silver pearlite or half silver, half copper are good color combinations. Tie the leader lengths according to the instructions on the package. For the six-inch size 0/0 Les Davis Herring Dodger the distance of the leader from the weight or downrigger should be only 24 inches and from the dodger to the bait or lure should be 16 inches. Measure these accurately and cut and retie if you are more than a half-inch long or short.

Use some method of removing or masking your human scent before handling the bait and you will get more hook-ups. Wash in a scent-free soap (such as Boraxo) or, better yet, smash up a baitfish and smear its oil on your fingertips and on your leader.

When to Fish

Throughout the season, fishing can be hot for a few days followed by a slow period so it's best to get the latest fishing reports when planning a trip. However, some months are generally better than others. The most consistent limits are caught when the season first opens. However these fish are smaller than late-season salmon and frequent storms may keep you off the ocean many days. June and July produce more limits than any other months and May and August have a mix of very good fishing with some slow times.

Early-season fishing off our West Coast is typically best south of San Francisco with Monterey Bay often the hot spot. By late spring, the center of the action shifts north to the San Francisco area while the Monterey area may continue to produce good catches throughout the summer.

Anglers can select from party boats but my favorite fishing is in a seaworthy private boat. Here catching fish requires cooperation and teamwork by everyone on the boat to bait the hooks or select lures, deploy lines in an efficient pattern, select the trolling speed, find the salmon, tend lines, play the hooked fish, pilot the boat and net the fish. In contrast, on a party boat you only tend your lines and play the fish.

Separate your lines by using a variety of weights and maybe downriggers. Use heavier weights on forward lines to take these lines down at a steep angle and light weights on aft lines so they trail farther behind the boat.

Whole frozen anchovies or fresh bait and jigs dressed with a filet of baitfish are about equally effective. The bait must be dead to stay on the barbless hooks required for salmon fishing which negates any action that a fresh bait could provide.

Good weather is a key to catching these fish. Safety is the first and most important concern and it just plain isn't safe with high winds or high seas. GPS or LORAN is required (not by law but for safety). Fishing is also easier and more successful with a low wind and fairly flat ocean. However, the best fishing weather is not bright sun and glassy smooth seas; an overcast sky combined with a slight wind ripple on the water make for ideal fishing conditions.

CHAPTER **4**

Back-Troll for Salmon and Trout in Rivers

Back-trolling for salmon and trout is a very effective fishing technique in rivers. Almost everyone who fishes for salmon from a boat on a river back-trolls. Many trout and steelhead anglers also use this method on large rivers. The largest sport-caught salmon on record—a 97-pound 4-ounce king salmon—was caught by Les Anderson's back-trolling on the Kenai River in Alaska.

This form of fishing is motoring against the current with the boat speed slower than the current in the river and the boat inching backwards. A variation is to anchor and let out line allowing the current to give the lure its action, or troll slightly faster than the current moving slowly upriver.

Anglers back-troll in rivers in California, Oregon, Washington, British Columbia and Alaska, and I suspect most rivers that hold salmon. Rivers like the Sacramento, Feather, Trinity, Klamath and Smith in California; the Alseas, Chetco, Nehalem, Rogue and Umpqua in Oregon, the Columbia, Cowlitz and Lewis in Washington and the Kanektok, Kenai, Kvichak, Lost Creek, Naknek and Mulchatna in Alaska are ideal for back-trolling for salmon, trout or steelhead.

West Coast salmon stop eating when they enter their rivers to spawn—they will die after spawning so no longer need food. Tempting them with food imitations doesn't generally work. At this time salmon need to be irritated

Guide Larry Suiter, John Skrabo and Butch King with a salmon caught back-trolling on the Naknek River in Alaska.

into striking. A strike may be an abrupt, arm-jarring take when fishing a lure, but it will more likely be soft and not obvious—mouthing the lure or bait may be a better description. The take is particularly soft when fishing bait.

Salmon will take wobble lures like Kwikfish, Flatfish or Magnum Wiggle Warts. They still seem to respond to scent and attaching a sardine fillet on the lure helps draw takes. They will also take cured roe—though I don't know why.

The bait or lure is moving slowly, zigzagging back and forth across the fishing hole, working slowly downstream. A salmon resting in the deep pool can see and smell the lure or bait coming, feel the vibrations and need only open its mouth to take the offering as it approaches. Ideally the lure or bait is right in the salmon's face; the fish should have to move out of the lure's path. Perhaps it

23

will be irritated just enough to mouth it. If you sense the fish quickly enough and set the hook, you have the fish on your line.

Salmon on the Feather River

I fished with guide Buck Arden and another angler on the Feather River in Northern California in early October last year. Arden motored down river and nosed his flat-bottomed water jet-powered boat into shore

An angler fights a large king salmon.

to set up tackle. He filleted a sardine, shaped the fillets to match the underside of the Kwikfish lures we would be using and secured a fillet to each lure by making two dozen wraps of thread around the combination.

We moved to the head of a hole. Arden told us how to let out line and find the bottom as he set up a back-trolling pattern. Occasionally a salmon would jump or roll on the surface but seeing them doesn't always mean catching them. Some guides fish and hook most of the fish but Arden didn't fish; instead he taught us how to hook our own fish—it was up to us to work the lure or bait, feel the bite and set the hook. Then it was "us against the fish" aided by Arden's skillful boat handling and expert instructions.

After an hour back-trolling, I felt a resistance when I lifted my rod. I didn't know if it was a salmon but set the hook. The rod arched over and I started to reel. "You got one," Arden yelled, "reel fast." By that time, the fish was running downstream. I held the rod tip high and got ready to reel when the fish turned. Soon it was coming upstream and I reeled as fast as I could. Arden maneuvered the boat to keep the salmon off the port side of the boat. As the salmon tired, Arden got the net ready and let the boat drift. We were downstream well below where I hooked the fish when Arden plunged the net in front of the tired fish and lifted it out of the water.

Arden estimated the fish weighed 15 pounds. I had decided to release my fish so we took pictures quickly, then put the fish back into the net and into the water so it could recuperate. After a couple more pictures, Arden twisted the hooks on the Kwikfish out of the fish's mouth and put the salmon back in the water, holding it until the fish was revived enough to swim from his grip.

A couple hours later, after we switched to roe—the fishing procedure with lures and roe is the same—I felt a resistance and set the hook. The bite may be soft on a lure but it is just light pressure on roe. The rod bent and line started coming off the reel. Arden netted this hen that was a bit larger than my first fish. We photographed and released the fish to continue her spawning journey.

How to Fish

The Feather River has shallow riffles so the best way to fish this river is from a drift boat or a shallow draft boat with a water jet-drive. In this boat you can fish the full length of the river.

24

Salmon conserve their energy by resting on the bottom in deep holes where the current is slow, so the bait or lure must be on or very near the bottom. If the lure hangs up on the bottom, water drag on the line will maintain a force on the line and it isn't obvious that the lure is caught. "If you lose contact with the bottom, you must reel in your line until you are sure your lure or bait is swimming free and drop down until you feel it make contact," Arden said. Maintaining contact with the bottom means repeatedly lifting the lure or bait off the bottom and setting it back down. You must feel it tap down on each drop. If it doesn't tap bottom, your lure is probably snagged.

To make matters a little more complicated, you want to keep the rod low to the water as you lift your lure or bait. You often detect a strike by feeling pressure as you lift the rod. If your rod is too high when a salmon strikes, you have no way to set the hook. You are constantly taking in a crank or two on your reel handle or letting a little line out to keep contact with the bottom and keeping your rod low. You should lift the lure only a few inches then set it back down but each time you must feel it bump the bottom. How well you do this and keep your lure bouncing along the bottom with your rod in position to set the hook will largely determine how many fish you catch.

Some rivers have a smooth bottom that doesn't usually snag the lure or bait. Here you can just let out to bottom every couple of minutes and need not bounce bottom. You don't need to think about line profile through the water or how deep you are fishing, just concentrate on feeling the bottom. Any time something feels different, set the hook. It may be a snag but it may also be a fish.

Kvichak Trophy Trout

Rainbow trout in the Kvichak River in Alaska have a plentiful, year-round food supply of salmon eggs and salmon smolt and grow to monstrous size. They live and feed in the 100-mile-long, deep, food-rich Lake Iliamna during the winter. Here decent-sized means at least a seven- or eight-pound trout. I wanted to catch a 10-pound trout on a fly rod but fly fished three days on this

Cured roe fished off a weight is the favorite bait for salmon.

river and had not landed a decent-sized trout. I had one half day left and I knew I would have my best chance trolling with conventional gear so I decided to pack up my fly rod and fish with the lodge's trolling tackle.

My guide completely agreed with my decision. He was relieved because he knew trolling would give me the best chance to catch a large trout. After a quick breakfast, we motored the half mile to the mouth of the river to troll. I selected a silver and brass Les Davis Canadian Wonder Spoon and we started fishing.

The trolling procedure was to barely inch forward against the current letting the flowing water generate the lure action. My guide gave the boat a slight angle into the current and we slid laterally to fish a wide area as we slowly moved forward.

The first pass along the north shore netted a pink salmon. I still hadn't caught a large trout. The second pass I had another hit and it only took a second to know what I had. The large silver fish jumped straight up, its body perfectly vertical; a couple of seconds later it was up in the air again with a repeat performance. After four jumps it stayed deep. The fish's intensity took its toll and ten minutes later the trout was at the side of the boat. My guide netted the 11-pound trout—I had caught my 10-pound trout with a pound to spare. After a couple of quick photos, my guide twisted the hook out of its mouth, held the fish in the current a few seconds and the trout spurted away.

We repeated the trolling pattern and I caught an eight-pound trout. We trolled on the other side of the river and hooked and landed another. I hooked a trout almost every pass. Other anglers were landing fish but not nearly as many as I was landing. My lure must have been just what the trout wanted that morning and the trolling pattern my guide set up was perfect for the fish.

Five hours after we started, I had to catch my airplane. I had hooked 11 trout and landed nine. Their average weight was about 10 pounds. The largest measured 33 inches long and

A guide shows off a large rainbow trout caught back-trolling the Naknek River.

weighed about 13 pounds. My frustration the first three days had evaporated and I felt a deep respect and appreciation for these large, hard-fighting trout. I was very lucky to be fishing the Kvichak River during the brief time these fish were in the river.

Trout and steelhead are different from salmon. Steelhead will return to spawn over and over and trout are resident in the rivers. Both are eating and will take a lure as food. Now you need to imitate a baitfish or at least some form of food. The lure need not always be on the bottom as the fish will move to take a meal. But most fish will be in the slower-moving water at the bottom so the lure should be deep to attract fish.

Bait, Boat and Tackle

A light- to medium-weight freshwater rod with 10-pound-test line is a good outfit for large trout. Kick that up to a medium-weight rod and 15-pound-test line for large Alaska trout. A medium- to heavyweight rod with 20- to 30-pound-test line is good for king salmon. A spinning reel is fine for smaller fish but a conventional revolving spool reel has fewer moving parts, a better drag system and is more reliable. It is almost required for salmon and is a better choice for trout and steelhead.

I have used conventional monofilament line but next year I will try low stretch, ultra-sensitive fusion or super braid lines. Sensitivity to feel the bait or lure, reduced water drag due to their small line diameters and low stretch when trying to make a forceful hook-set are all advantages.

In Alaska, silver or silver and bronze spoons like size 2/0 Canadian Wonders and Pixees are good lures for trolling for trout in shallow rivers. Hot Shots or Wiggle Warts are good for salmon or trout in deeper rivers. Magnum Wiggle Warts are tops in Alaska for salmon.

The most popular lures for salmon in California and the Pacific Northwest are large sardine-wrapped size T50 or M2 Flatfish or size K14 or K15 Kwikfish. A glob of cured roe wrapped onto a treble hook and held securely by taking several wraps of thread around the roe and hook is a very popular bait for salmon. Lures are favored in some rivers and roe is more popular in others. Wiggle Warts or its big cousin, Magnum Wiggle Warts and Hot Shots are good trout lures. Popular colors are red, gold and white, silver and yellow or combinations of these colors.

Specialized boats are best for different types of rivers. If the river is not too fast, a drift boat is a wonderful craft. A skilled rower can maneuver these boats to fish all of the holes and set them up for exciting shoots through white water. This is a trip with nature. The only sounds are flowing water, oars quietly dipping into the water and the call of birds.

An aluminum fishing boat with a conventional outboard motor is adequate if the part of the river you will fish is deep. By planning your fishing area, you can often fish a section of the river between riffles and use a conventional fishing boat. But for fishing in areas with shallow spots, a shallow draft, flat-bottomed boat—a type often called a sled—is ideal. The bottom of the boat is heavy aluminum to take the occasional scraping of the bottom as the boat goes over shallow areas. A water jet outdrive is required to negotiate shallow rivers.

Back-trolling is a great river fishing method. If you fish rivers for salmon from a boat, you will likely back-troll; if you are fishing large rivers for trout, back-trolling or slowly trolling forward against the current are very productive fishing methods. Most river guides back-troll to catch salmon and many use this method for trout. The best way to learn how to catch these fish is to make a trip with a guide, then decide if this is a type of fishing you want to do on your own.

Sam Waller, manager of Jot's Resort on the Rogue River, shows off two king salmon he caught back-trolling.

CHAPTER 5

High-Speed Trolling for Exotic Ocean Game Fish

Most of this book is devoted to freshwater fishing or trolling for anadromous fish like salmon and striped bass. For all of these fish, the trolling speed is slow and the main difference is that saltwater fish are usually larger, the bait or lure bigger and the line and tackle heavier. But there is a very different form of trolling for the speedster fish in the ocean—fast trolling. The speed can be six to ten knots or more; it covers many tens of miles of ocean in a day and is a basic way to find many of the saltwater fish.

These fish are warm-water pelagic fish that have no home but make annual circuits over large areas of the ocean seeking out small fish for food. They include marlin, sailfish, dorado, wahoo and all the tuna (albacore, bluefin, bigeye,

High-speed trolling catches hard-fighting game fish off Baja, Mexico.

skipjack and yellowfin). Typical baitfish they pursue include herring, anchovies, sardines and mackerel. These game fish swim very fast and nothing can outrun them—not a baitfish and not a lure trolled at high speed. While most freshwater fish swim no faster than 10 mph and salmon top out at about 15 mph, wahoo, sailfish and marlin can swim faster than 50 mph and the tuna family can approach this speed.

For school fish—tuna, dorado, yellowtail and wahoo—the idea is to locate and attract them by trolling. The school will stay with the hooked fish and seem to go into a feeding frenzy. The angler or anglers that hook the fish apply a lot of force to bring the fish to the boat. In the meantime, members of the crew chum with live bait. Bait is tossed one or two fish at a time into the water and the school of fish home-in on these baitfish. Then anglers cast live bait or lures to the fish.

Metal or plastic lures with bright colored skirts skip along the surface, sometimes alternating above water and just below water at these high trolling speeds. Large lures designed for high speed are trolled below the surface.

On the West Coast and in Hawaii, people in large private boats pursue these fish; anglers go on long-range sport fishing boats out of San Diego or from some Mexican ports. Others fish from private boats or take day-trips out of Southern California, the East Coast and Caribbean ports, Mexico, other Central or South American ports, Hawaii and Australia.

This isn't just trolling blind. Experienced skippers know where these fish have been found in recent years and where fish have been landed. Water temperature is a key so they look for the right water temperature for the species they are seeking. Albacore want water 62 degrees or warmer; yellowfin tuna need water that is above 69 degrees; yellowtail are looking for the same temperature; and wahoo are found in water above 70

A variety of lures like these are trolled at high speed to attract tuna.

degrees. Good fish finders are essential to decide when a school is large and should be fished and when to keep trolling. These are clues to a starting point but the key to finding fish is fast trolling to cover large expanses of ocean.

Deep, High-Speed Trolling

A new method to catch these fish has evolved over recent years—trolling at high speed with downriggers. Lures like Speedster and Marauders or Magnum Rapalas are taken to depth with downriggers.

The hydrodynamic forces on the weight, line and lure are great and the downrigger cable is swept back at a large angle. The depth of the trolled lure is only a fraction of the depth shown on the downrigger. Until now anglers guessed the lure depth, but the graphs in Chapter

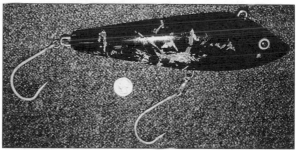

A marauder is a favorite lure for trolling for wahoo (note the teeth marks on the lure from a wahoo attack).

11 show the depth trolled for weight and downrigger setups at any speed up to 10 mph.

Gaudy Lures are Best

Lures are either bright colored to attract fish or colors that imitate food fish for the quarry. Favorite skirted lures are zucchini (they are the color of the vegetable), and Mexican Flag lures that are yellow, red, blue and white (the color of the

Mexican flag). Mackerel in various shades of blue or green and the dorado are favorite imitations of fish. Red and white, orange and black, purple or other bright colors are also good colors. Typical high-speed diving lures include Marauders, Speedster or ten pin lures from Braid, Yo Zuri Bonita Trolling Lure or Magnum Rapalas.

Fast-swimming fish see the action probably equating the lures to a school of baitfish at the surface and attack at high speed. Each marlin, sailfish or other large surface-feeding fish is a prize and catching even one is an accomplishment. Trolling is the usual fishing method. School fish like the tuna family, yellowtail, wahoo and dorado are often located trolling, then chumming with live bait keeps them near the boat and live bait or lures are used to catch them.

The depth of the lure usually isn't very important but they typically run very shallow. These fish do not have swim bladders that expand and disable other fish as they change depth; they can dive or climb to the surface in an instant.

More lures in the water don't necessarily mean more fish in the boat; sometimes only three lures and rarely more than four or five are trolled. Most anglers wait for a hookup and then fish with live bait or heavy lures to catch more fish from the school.

Warm-water Fish

Along our West Coast, the currents divide off Point Conception west of Santa Barbara. Warm currents flow south and cool currents flow north. Generally warm-water fish are found south of this point, and cool-water fish are north.

This isn't a perfect division as salmon, a cool-water fish, make a sweep south and albacore, a fish preferring moderate temperatures, is often found north all the way to Washington. Tuna and yellowtail are usually caught as far north as San Diego; dorado are usually found farther south and wahoo and sailfish are caught off the southern part of the Baja Peninsula.

An angler shows off his 125-pound yellowfin tuna.

Tackle for trolling should be heavy. The fish are not deterred by the heavy leaders though light line may be required to get hookups when casting bait or lures. Heavy wire leaders are used for wahoo since they have super sharp teeth that can shear monofilament line in two as if it were a piece of cooked spaghetti. Hooks on trolling lures are large, often double hooks, and have large barbs. Fish going tens of knots hit one of these lures, the drag on the reel is set tight and the large, strong hook is driven into the fish's jaw past the barb. Most fish hooked on troll are held securely and are landed.

If the school of fish is large, anglers may fish for hours catching fish from

30

that school. However, really large schools are unusual—typically a few fish are caught on bait after a school is located.

Some anglers only catch these fish on troll. Abe and Angelo Cuanang fishing alone in Boston Whalers troll several rods for albacore and may get multiple hookups. When they have several fish hooked, they stop, back the drags off on all but one reel and these fish stop fighting. They land one fish; take the next rod from its holder tighten the drag and land a second fish, and continue until all of the fish are landed. I am surprised these unattended fish don't take out yards and yards of line and get tangled, but the Cuanangs have learned these fish stop fighting when they loosen the drag. They can single-handedly land several fish that were all hooked at the same time.

Even with the best gear, catching a large tuna is a test of endurance. Tuna are super fighters with the greatest strength and stamina of any fish I have caught. They swim at very high speed and sound when they are hooked. Stopping a 200-pound tuna before it runs all the line off the reel is a challenge for any angler. Most anglers catch them stand-up fishing and all they have going for them is good tackle, a belt to hold the butt of the rod, a kidney harness and their strength and stamina.

Fish are hooked and going different directions so the skipper doesn't follow individual fish. You must apply a lot of force to move the fish to the boat. Even then, as Helen Springer found after fighting a 100-pound tuna for 30 minutes aboard the *Royal Star*, doing everything right, the line, frayed from the battle, snapped as the big fish came into view. It was only seconds away from the gaff.

Wahoo are equally challenging but in a different way. It may take days of searching to find a few wahoo but finding and catching wahoo is completely different. Even on a bite, their hard bony mouths resist hook-ups and their sharp teeth cut through lines. But some are hooked solidly and are landed.

Kelp Paddies are Key

Kelp paddies, or even a small piece of debris in the ocean, are often the key to finding fish. This small discontinuity in the vast open ocean often is enough to attract a school of fish. The size of the paddy doesn't relate to the number of fish it holds. *Royal Star* crew member Brian Sims said they have seen large kelp paddies with no fish and a mile away a very small kelp paddy holding a large school of fish.

Brian Sims lands a wahoo.

When trolling and searching for kelp paddies, one crew member is in the crow's nest with binoculars scanning the horizon looking for a kelp paddy or a piece of small debris. This person high above the water has the advantage and

31

usually spots one first but the skipper and other members of the crew also have binoculars and are searching the horizon all around the boat.

Kelp paddies are sparse; a few are dispersed in hundreds of square miles of ocean. On a good day, the crew may spot eight or ten small, table-top-sized kelp paddies. Hours of searching can pay off suddenly when one is spotted that holds many fish. Skippers take advantage of reports from other boats, their knowledge of the sea and their intuition to find kelp. Paddies drift with the current and wind and may move many miles in a day. Skippers with the best knowledge of winds and currents, the most persistence and some luck find the best kelp paddies and catch the most fish.

Tackle

These fish give new meaning to the requirement for premium tackle. Most fish don't tax gear to the limit, but these fish do. The reel must be a quality reel with a good drag and it must be in excellent condition. Premium reels like the two-speed Penn International, Shimano Tiagra or Finn Nor are needed for the largest fish. For small fish in the 50-pound-class or less, good quality saltwater reels like Penn Senators, Newells, Shimanos or Diawas are suitable. For intermediate 100-pound-class fish, Shimano two-speed reels like TLDII 30s are sufficient, and are less expensive and lighter than the top-of-the-line reels.

Trolling rigs should be stout outfits with 80-pound-test line (60- or 100-pound line is okay). Choose a short, heavy (5 1/2- to 6-foot rod) so you have the greatest leverage to fight a fish. I use Fenwick, Penn and Seeker rods but Calstar and Sabre rods are also good.

You need a Marauder-type lure for trolling for wahoo. These large lures are hit by wahoo when feathers and plastic trolling jigs are ignored. Heavy nylon leaders are okay for most fish, but for wahoo, use a heavy, five-foot-long wire leader—275-pound-test strength wire is about right. All rigging for wahoo should be black. A wahoo may hit a bright chrome swivel or ring between the line and leader and bite the monofilament in two at the connection.

You want quality line so you don't break off a large fish. Izorline, Berkley Big Game, Maxima and Fenwick Saltline are some of the quality lines made for tough offshore ocean fishing and are good for trolling. You need a quality rod belt and a kidney harness in case you hook a large tuna. I use a Braid Brute Buster belt and harness that can handle large fish.

Long-range Fishing Boats

Long-range fishing is an excellent way to catch fast exciting game fish. About a dozen boats make long-range fishing trips out of San Diego. Most have state-rooms for two or three people, serve excellent meals and all catch fish. Typical rooms have a closet, half a dozen drawers or shelves, a sink with hot and cold running water and an electrical outlet. Several showers on the boat mean little waiting to clean up after a day of fishing.

For more information, contact the *Royal Star*, *Royal Polaris* and the *Shogun* at 629/226-8030. For the *Excel*, *Searcher* and the *Polaris Supreme* call Fisherman's Landing at 619/221-8500. Point Loma Sportfishing charters the *American Angler*, the *Qualifier 105* and the *Vagabond*. Call them at 619/223-1627 for information and reservations. H&M Landing at 619/222-1144 charters *The Spirit of Adventure* and the *Big Game 90*. The *Red Rooster III* is chartered out of Lee Palm Sportfishing at 619/224-3857.

Baja Mexico locations have similar long-range fishing boats and East Coast, Central and South American ports also use high speed trolling for the premium game fish.

CHAPTER 6

Trolling Catches the Most Fish

Almost any game fish can be caught trolling. If a fish eats other fish, and most game fish do, a moving lure that imitates a bait will catch it. Fish ranging in size from small crappies to giant marlin and sailfish are caught trolling. The most popular Western offshore fish (salmon) to the most popular freshwater fish (trout and black bass) are caught trolling, Walleye, pike and muskellunge, the fastest fish in the ocean (wahoo), and the hardest-fighting (tuna), striped bass, kokanee (landlocked sockeye salmon), halibut and many other species are caught trolling.

Even catfish, rockfish and lingcod are occasionally caught on trolled bait or lures, but this isn't the best way to catch these fish and isn't the usual fishing method for them.

This angler caught these striped bass trolling a lure at San Luis Reservoir in California.

Trolling Catches Bass

Classic black bass fishing is motoring along the shoreline with a trolling motor casting to tulles and rocks and under docks or working shale banks for smallmouth and spotted bass. I have caught bass while trolling for trout, usually off a shallow point, but it has been by accident. Matt DeSimone, a skilled bass angler using classical casting techniques, put away his casting rods and trolls for bass during the warmer months and made some of his best catches. Here is how he did it.

"In warm weather, bass will hug the shoreline in shallow water very early in the day and conventional bass fishing methods are best, but as sunlight falls on the water, bass move deeper," DeSimone said. "Then you need to move away from the shoreline to find them. Look for bass or baitfish on your fish finder. During these warm days, you will find bass around underwater humps in eight to 15 feet of water early and deeper later in the day. Trolling is an excellent way to catch them."

I trolled for bass with Matt, his father Bill, and his son Matthew at Lake Del Valle near Livermore, California. We started trolling the shallow south end of this lake and had only been trolling a few minutes when my silver Rat-L-Trap was hit. I landed and released a small largemouth bass about 10 inches long. Soon Bill had another small one. I hooked and lost one; then Matthew caught a legal-sized fish. Matt was running the boat, watching the fish finder, following depth contours and not fishing. Matt said we could do better and moved to another area called the Narrows.

We caught a few more fish including a four-pound catfish—an advantage of trolling for bass is that other species including large trout will also take the typical bass lures. On our next move we caught a 6.3-pound trout and later caught a squawfish (not considered a game fish but a good fighter on light tackle).

By midday we wanted to try one last time at the southern end of the lake before we quit fishing. Matthew tied on a black-backed, silver Fat "A". He barely got the lure out when he had a hit. A couple minutes later he had another and was letting out line a third time when he caught another fish. All these fish caught in about 10 minutes were small, either sub-legal or marginally legal. We landed about 25 bass in a half day, enough to convince me that trolling for black bass can be very productive.

DeSimone trolled fast—about 3 mph. "We get a lot of reaction strikes and I want bass to have only enough time to react." He varied his speed both slower and faster to see what velocity drew the most strikes.

A fish finder is essential. These fish follow the bait so find bait on the fish finder and you will probably find bass. The bait and thus the fish are often in the same area from day to day and from year to year. We were seeing schools of bait much of the time and we fished where we saw bait.

We fished with a variety of lures but the black-backed, silver Rebel Fat "A" was the top lure and the Rat-L-Trap was second. Other fish were caught on a shad rap, and a Wee R. Other good lures include the Poe 400 series to get deep, and the Wiggle Wart series.

Sometimes you can use a lure that dives almost to the bottom. Let line out until the lure is ticking the bottom; then reel in line to get the lure above the bottom and above the bass. The eyes of bass and other fish are positioned to look to the side and up. They don't see what is under them so the lure should be at their level or above them to draw a strike. You don't want to go too deep.

A change in velocity will often trigger a strike so changing speed is also an important part of this strategy.

Retrieving Snagged Lures

Any time you are trolling along the bottom, whether you are fishing for bass or other species, you are going to occasionally hang your lure on rocks, a ledge or a sunken tree. Usually you circle back and try to shake it free, then just break it off if it is hooked solid. When you are fishing near the bottom you can expect several hookups on the bottom and several lost lures in a day. You can retrieve almost every snagged lure with a heavy lure retriever.

We used six-pound-test line so couldn't apply very much force to the fish or a snag. We hooked our lures on the bottom or on submerged trees eight or ten times during the day. About half came free by trolling back over the lure and shaking it free. The other half were recovered by slipping the lure retriever over the line, dropping it down to the lure and working it up and down until the chains on the retriever caught the hooks on the lure and the lure could be pulled away from the snag.

Striped Bass

Striped bass are usually caught on bait. In the San Francisco Bay the standard fishing method is drifting live bait. Along ocean beaches, anglers cast bait or various large lures to catch them. In the Sacramento Delta butterfly-cut shad, bullheads or mudsuckers are the top baits. Sometimes stripers are caught fishing bait off ocean piers.

But often trolling is the best method to catch striped bass both in saltwater and freshwater. I trolled with guide Chuck Hostetler at New Hogan Reservoir trolling large Rapalas, jointed Rebels and Rat-L-Trap lures about 150 feet behind our boat. We weren't using weight—just letting the diving force of the lure take the lure down to a shallow depth. By trolling around islands and in shallow areas in the lake we were able to entice stripers to strike and caught six stripers in three hours of fishing.

Trolling is also a good fishing method in the San Francisco Delta and in saltwater or brackish estuaries. These stripers are caught on the same lures used in lakes. However, a favorite fishing method here is using a wire spreader, attaching a big crankbait on one leg and a metal spoon on the other, or a spoon on one and a Hair Raiser or Bugeye Jig on the other. Rapala, Bombers, Rat-L-Traps, solid or jointed Rebels and Hopkins Jigs all catch striped bass trolling.

Striped bass are a particularly wary fish. Some anglers forego gasoline-powered engines using only electric trolling motors to minimize the disturbance and avoid spooking these fish. Also, long line out behind the boat gets good separation and doesn't spook the fish—guide Barry Canavero trolls his lures 200 feet behind the boat. Trolling in large "S" curves so lures take a different track than the boat is also a good practice.

Stripers need to be active to chase and strike a trolled bait. As the water temperature cools, a striper's metabolism slows down. They become lethargic and don't attack a trolled lure. Canavero says his break point for trolling is 56 degrees. He often trolls when the water temperature is warmer than 56 degrees but he always anchors and fishes bait if the water is cooler.

John Skrabo landed this striped bass trolling a crankbait on a lake.

Walleye

Randy Brudnicki describes three ways to troll for walleye. Walleyes are nomadic fish traveling in schools, so trolling is a good way to intercept these schools. Once a school is located anglers may catch several fish. Troll very slowly along the bottom using a night crawler or a minnow for bait. At this slow speed, it doesn't take much weight to reach the depth you need and one-half to one ounce of weight is usually sufficient. A five- to seven-foot-long leader is used to separate the bait from the weight.

You should be just inching along and sometimes a form of back-trolling is used for walleye as a way to slow down. The engine is operated in reverse and the boat is traveling stern first. A boat will troll more slowly going backwards for two reasons. First the stern of the boat heading into the water pushes a lot of water compared with the sleek bow cutting through the water. Also, motors are sometimes geared lower in reverse and the prop and lower units are less efficient in reverse so the motor doesn't apply as much thrust.

Pushing a boat with a motor at slow speed on windy days makes steering difficult. I've had days trolling at normal speed where the wind continuously blew the boat off course. I would need to accelerate, steer back to course, then slow down to trolling speed. Steering at slow speed is easier when the motor is pulling a boat through the water—bass boats have their trolling motors on the bow for easy steering. Pulling it stern-first through the water is different but on breezy days it is easier to steer backwards than it is to troll very slowly bow-first.

A disadvantage of this backward trolling is that waves lap over the back of the boat rather than being cut by the bow. You are much more likely to get water in the boat going backwards so this works best on relatively calm days with low waves.

When walleye are hunkered down in protected areas like weed beds, a strategy is to get a reaction strike. Speed-trolling a Rapala or spinner two to 3 mph just over the weeds will often draw these fish from their cover.

A third trolling method is bottom-bouncing at an intermediate speed. A spinner rig is typically used on an L-shaped spreader. It usually takes two- or three-ounce weights to get the lure down to the bottom at this velocity.

Kokanee Salmon

Kokanee are landlocked sockeye salmon and are generally small, averaging less than 12 inches in length though some will grow to 18 to 20 inches. These are usually stocked as small fingerlings—thousands of small fingerlings can be stocked in a lake at low cost. The survival rate is not high but it is high enough to yield a good return on the investment. They do most of their growing in the lake, are well-acclimated and fight like wild fish.

To catch kokanee, think of them as trout except run your lure about 10 feet deeper—if you are catching trout, add enough weight to troll 10 feet deeper. A wedding ring lure tipped with canned corn is a standard fishing lure. Needlefish or a variety of other small lures are also effective. Lead-core line is a favorite way to fish for them but trolling with a light lure and a weight is also a good fishing method.

Mackinaw

Mackinaw or lake trout are caught trolling and this is a special kind of trolling. These are cold-water fish favoring a 46 to 48 degree water temperature. They are usually found near the bottom in large, deep lakes such as the Great Lakes, Lake Tahoe in California and Nevada, Lake Odell and Crescent Lake in Oregon and Flaming Gorge Reservoir in Utah and Wyoming. Fishing depths of 100 to 300 feet are typical but early in the season, right after ice-out, or in the cold lakes in the far north, like Big Bear Lake and Slave Lake in Canada, they may be caught near the surface in shallow water.

When lake trout are found on the bottom (most of the year) anglers fish areas in a lake that have a smooth bottom. They lower their rigs all the way to the bottom and troll with the lure or bait bouncing along or very near bottom.

When fish are deep, the fishing method is usually trolling with wire leaders or with downriggers. Chris Turner of Clear Water Guide Service at Lake Tahoe fishes some rigs with braided wire line and fishes others with super line, like Berkeley Fireline, off downriggers. Live minnows threaded onto a hook or lures like Rapalas are favorite attractors. Sometimes a large flasher or dodger is used in front of the bait.

Wire Line

Steel line is a very dense line—almost eight times as dense as water. It sinks quickly making it ideal for deep-water trolling. Still, trolling on the bottom at a depth of 150 feet may require 300 feet or more of line out to reach the bottom even at slow trolling speed. Wire line also has very little stretch so it is very sensitive to a bite. Anglers can set a hook even fishing with a long line.

Wire line kinks easily and is difficult to handle. You don't cast wire line but simply let it flow out from the reel. Patience is required—let line out slowly and don't let the reel spool spin very fast. Wire line can create a really nasty backlash and can spoil a fishing trip. Wire line is either a solid, single strand or multi-strand. Single strand line is more dense and sinks at a steeper angle because multistrand line has a certain amount of void space in the line.

Almost any fish you are after can be caught trolling. The next time you go for your favorite fish, consider trolling as a fishing method.

The author caught this striped bass trolling a Rat-L-Trap lure at New Hogan Reservoir.

CHAPTER 7

Lead-core Line Catches Fish

A lure or a light weight and lure trolled on a given line at a given speed will only troll so deep. After it reaches that depth, letting more line out doesn't increase its depth. For light lures this is very shallow, sometimes only a few feet under the surface.

Using downriggers, adding weight to your line or trolling a heavy or deep-diving lure, gets your line deeper but using weighted line is another good way to go deep. Lead-core line is the weighted line most used in freshwater fishing and is a simple solution. You don't need the expense, extra weight and complication of a downrigger. You can use lead-core line on any boat including a friend's boat or on a rental boat.

Advantage of Lead-core

The trolled depth with this line varies with trolling velocity and the depth is directly related to the amount of line you spool out. If you are fishing 12 feet deep with two colors of lead-core line (the color changes every 10 yards so two colors is 20 yards or 60 feet of line), you will get to a depth of 24 feet when you let out four colors, 36 feet with 6 colors and 60 feet with 10 colors. To fish deeper with monofilament line, you reel in and change weights; to fish deeper with lead-core, you need only let out more line.

The troll depth depends on the boat speed and graphs in Chapter 11 show how deep you are trolling for a typical lead-core line at various trolling speeds. As you troll slowly, lead-core goes very deep, but at moderate speeds, it is shallow.

Great Lure Presentation

Lead-core makes an excellent presentation to the fish. The lure is trolled far behind the boat at a controlled depth. The bait or lure is separated from the line

by a long leader— 30 or 40 feet is not too long. Add two colors or 60 feet of lead-core out and the lure is 90 to 100 feet behind the boat.

Let's visualize what a fish sees. First the boat passes over the fish and it may be alerted. Now 60 feet of heavy line slips

Peter and Valerie Liebold troll for trout using lead-core line.

through the water but that shouldn't be too scary to the fish. Next, separated by 30 or 40 feet, a bait or lure swims by seemingly disassociated from the rest of the gear, but of course attached by a fine leader. It is typically more than 30 seconds from the time the boat passes until the lure arrives—probably enough time for the fish to disassociate the two events and take the lure.

Another advantage of the long leader is that in the final part of the fight the lead-core line is all wound on the reel and the fish is played on the light leader. The leader slices through the water without a weight or a lot of line drag and it is a pleasure to fight the fish during the last phase of the fight. A light rod, a light drag setting on the reel and the light leader are optimum for playing the fish delicately.

Sometimes back at the dock after a day's fishing I've been greeted with the news that they weren't biting today until we open our fish box with a nice catch of fish. People usually ask, "Where were you fishing? What lure or bait were you using?" After this usually follows the most important questions, "How were you fishing and how deep were you fishing?"

Lead-core line is a low stretch line. I suspect the low stretch character of lead-core improves the percentage of hookups. I've also found I have had good success with new low stretch super lines. Low stretch lines may hook fish better than monofilament line.

Lead-core Description

Lead-core line is a lead wire encased in a braided line. Lead has a density 11.3 times the density of water so it sinks quickly. However, the density of the woven sleeve is about the same as water so the sink rate is reduced. The density of steel is 7.86 times the density of water, not as heavy as lead, but it needs no encasing line. As a result the steel line sinks faster.

Lead-core line comes in a variety of strengths—common lines have a strength of 12, 18 and 27 pounds. The two lighter strengths are most useful for typical freshwater fishing and the heavier is preferable for saltwater fishing.

Spinning reels aren't suitable for lead-core or wire line. The line makes an abrupt turn at the pick-up point on a spinning reel and these lines aren't flexible enough to make that turn. An Abu Garcia 5500 or similar level wind reel is ideal for lead-core line. I highly recommend the conventional reel but you can even use an inexpensive fly reel and put a hundred yards of backing and about three colors of lead-core line on the reel for trolling to about 20 feet deep.

If you need to get really deep, you will need a larger reel—probably a

A variety of strengths of lead-core line are supplied by several manufacturers.

saltwater reel—which holds a lot of line. Choose a fairly large reel (a size 3/0 is about right), with a high gear ratio retrieve. Large is best because the line is bulky and a high gear ratio speeds recovery of the long line.

I like a light rod and that works fine with this setup. My favorite for freshwater is a medium light, six-foot, six-inch-long rod designed for 6- to 12-pound-test line. A spinning rod is okay as long as you can mount the conventional reel on the reel holder.

Leader

With a monofilament line and a weight, your maximum practical leader length is about the length of the rod. The weight stops at the end of the rod and you can't get a fish close enough to land if your leader length is excessive. With a short leader, the weight creates a disturbance near the lure that makes the bait or lure appear less natural. (I'll suggest a way to avoid this problem by getting more separation between the weight and lure in Chapter 15.)

Since no weight is involved with the weighted lines—the line is the weight—you can tie a very long leader to the end of your line. Tie a smooth knot like a nail knot or needle knot so the leader slips easily through the eyes on your rod and winds onto the reel.

The secret for lead-core line is the long leader and it must be long and light! I use at least a 30-foot-long leader and I usually use a six-pound-test leader for freshwater. If the water is very clear or the fish seem finicky, I may also tie on an additional 15 feet of four-pound-test leader. A fisherman with a 15-foot leader will catch fish, but an angler with a longer leader of the same strength will catch more fish. A 30-foot leader is effective and I believe a longer leader has little benefit. A two-pound leader may mean more hookups but I believe enough fish would be lost to negate any initial advantage. In addition, the larger fish that I want to catch have a better chance to break off with this very light line.

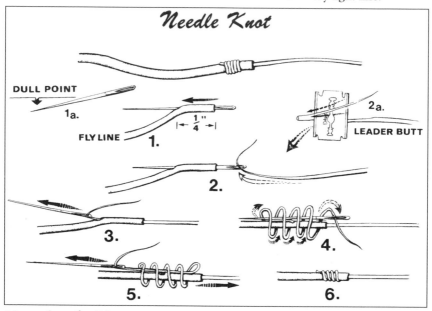

Managing the Line

A long leader combined with a light lure is a bit difficult to play out. Lead-core line kinks and backlashes so it is tricky to deploy. A light lure that is a very good fish attractor creates little drag to pull the line out and friction from the wet leader on the eyes of the rod may keep the line from slipping through the eyes at low trolling speeds. A combination of shaking the rod and swinging the rod in an arc to pull the lure through the water fast to apply an extra drag force will work the leader out. Another way to apply more force to help deploy the leader is to increase your trolling speed until the lead-core line comes through the eye on the tip of the rod and slips into the water. Once the heavy line is in the water, the trolling speed can be reduced and the line will run out fairly smoothly.

Be patient letting out this line. Lead-core line is awkward to play out but I have fished with anglers as young as five years old to a 90-year-old man who have both quickly learned to handle lead-core line. Keep your thumb on the spool of

40

the reel and pull out the line a few feet at a time. Don't let the spool turn too fast. With all of the weight of the lead, the reel spool has a lot of momentum, overruns and backlashes easily. Be patient and work the line out in a couple of minutes. The few minutes you lose in fishing time when putting out the line is a small part of the fishing day. So take your time and be certain your lure isn't tangled and you don't create a backlash.

Cathy Lambert landed this trout while trolling lead-core line in a Bay Area lake.

Lures

With this line, the lure doesn't need to have much drag so very light lures are practical. I like a size one Needlefish, a small Triple Teazer, a Dick Nite or other light lures. You can also use heavier lures like Kastmasters, Cripplures, Apex's, Z-Rays and crankbaits like Rapalas, Rat-L-Traps and Thundersticks but they will run deeper than the light lures. Small lures better imitate small baitfish found in most lakes so think small when selecting lures. Consider heavy lures and deep-diving crankbaits when you need to fish deep.

When to Use Lead-core Line

Often the surface is dimpled with the intermittent activity of fish as they chase bait to the surface and trout occasionally jump after baitfish. Does this mean you should be fishing on the surface? Probably not. In fact these are the conditions that produce some of the best catches with lead-core line trolled a few feet below the surface.

The main activity may be taking place a few feet down. Perhaps the action of the boat drives the fish down or maybe that is where trout are concentrated. But a lure trolled about 60 to 100 feet behind the boat and five to 10 feet deep is extremely effective around this surface activity.

Trolling is most effective and most sporting when the surface of the lake is cool and fish are shallow. In our cooler regions this may be in midsummer while in the temperate zone across much of the United States this occurs during fall, winter and early spring. During warmer times, cool-water fish are often deep well beneath this shallow range. A large reel full of line—a full 100-yard spool of line—will often reach them and competes with a downrigger as the preferred fishing technique.

Lead-core Salmon

Lead-core line can be used for any fish. Several years ago when we were trolling for salmon with heavy weights and heavy tackle, I started using lead-core line on a lighter rod. When we saw salmon on the fish finder at about 35 feet, I thought I needed about seven colors of lead-core line out. I threaded on a frozen and thawed anchovy and spooled out that number of colors of line.

The line was far behind other rigs and didn't interfere with other anglers' lines. Four of us set up our normal array of three rods trolled with heavy

41

weights and two lines off downriggers then added a sixth rod using lead-core line. (This was before we were restricted to one rod per angler.)

The first weekend I tried lead-core line for salmon, more than half the fish that we landed (five of the nine), including the two largest fish, were caught on lead-core. I was sure I had found a new secret to catching salmon. On subsequent trips, the lead-core usually caught its share of the fish and often more but it never again so dominated the catch.

The light rig made catching these fish a pleasure. On this rig, a salmon typically makes a run when it is hooked. Then it usually turns and heads toward the boat and the line goes slack. Be ready and don't quit reeling just because you don't feel tension on the line. The fish could be off but more likely, it is just swimming toward the boat. Reel fast to keep some tension in the line. When most of the lead-core line is on the reel, you usually begin to feel the fish again.

An anchovy, a fly or a lure are all good attractors. My goal is to make this presentation as natural as possible so I leave the gaudy attractors like dodgers or flashers for the lines close to the boat and troll only a lure or bait.

Some days salmon are evidently attracted by the boat and its wake and will hit a lure just behind the vessel. On other days, or at other times during the day, fish seem to avoid the lures under the boat and a lure far behind the boat on lead-core line is the rig that fish hit consistently.

A light rod, a rod that is well suited to fighting a salmon, will handle lead-core line. That also means no weights on sinker releases that are dropped to the bottom at each hookup, no extra cost for dropped weights and no running out of sinkers when you troll through school after school of undersized salmon.

Salmon trollers in other boats expect you will have all of your lines taken down with heavy weights at very steep angles behind your boat. They may cut across close to your stern and their lines will hook your lead-core line. You may need to reel in your long lead-core line quickly if another boat approaches too close. In crowded trolling conditions, it may be impractical to use this fishing method.

When bait hasn't produced hits on your lead-core line and you are tired of checking bait, switch to a lure. A bait that has been hit and torn up probably won't draw another strike but a lure will keep attracting fish even after it has been hit. You can almost ignore this line and lure until it has a fish.

Trolling with lead-core line is a very effective trolling method for all gamefish. A bait or lure trolled far behind the boat on a leadcore rig will fool many wary fish that would pass up lures or bait trolled close to the boat.

This salmon was caught in the ocean on lead-core line.

CHAPTER 8

Downriggers to Get Deep

Deep fish require special trolling tactics. You can use very heavy weights but that makes handling the gear difficult and still may not get your lure down deep enough. You can use lead-core or steel line, but downriggers are the best answer for most deep fish. You attach your bait or lure and crank the weight down to get really deep. Fifty feet, 100 feet or even 200 feet is a practical depth to troll.

The two primary advantages of a downrigger are getting very deep and trolling at a precise depth. Even when fish aren't exceptionally deep, this is an easy way to get your lure or bait precisely to their depth. Anglers are also finding this is a way to troll in lakes with floating weeds and debris without constantly fouling the lure.

Downriggers aren't a panacea. Get a downrigger cable caught in the prop in a rough sea, then get tossed around by the waves with no power to control the boat, as I did one time when fishing with a friend, and you will wonder if these are really such a great idea. Managing the extra gear of a downrigger in a small confined boat makes you feel like you need as many arms as an octopus to control the line, the downrigger, the trolling motor and the electronics.

The Basic Downrigger

In its simplest form, a downrigger is a heavy weight on the end of a cable with some attachment to connect the line on or near the weight. It has a spool to hold the cable and an arm to extend the cable out over the water beside or behind the boat. Except for real economy models, downriggers all have counters to show the length of line spooled out.

The counter is actually counting revolutions of the downrigger spool. One revolution equals a foot when the spool holding the cable is 3.82 inches in diameter—the standard-sized spool for most downriggers. So the indicator shows the number of feet of cable under water. For a normal slow trolling speed, the weight goes almost straight down and your counter shows your trolling depth.

This salmon was caught off a downrigger in the ocean.

Your line is attached to the weight or the cable above the weight with a clip. When a fish is hooked and pulls hard, the line releases from a clip so you have the luxury of playing the fish with no weight on your line.

The downrigger has some form of adjustable clutch like a star drag on a reel. Set the clutch tight enough to hold the weight but loose enough so the cable will play out if the weight gets caught on the bottom. You can then circle around and usually free the weight. If the downrigger clutch is set too tightly, the cable can pull that side of the boat down before you react to the problem, tipping the boat enough to fill it with water.

Downriggers range from small, simple, portable models that sell for as little as $50 to large, deluxe models costing several hundred dollars. Basic downriggers are hand-cranked up or down. More elaborate models are driven by electric motors and may have an extending arm to position the cable far away from the boat to keep the cable away from other lines and the prop on your boat.

Normally the hand-cranked models are fine but in really deep water the luxury of a motor to pull the downrigger is great. When fishing primarily for mackinaw in deep water, Chris Turner, who guides at Lake Tahoe, uses motor-driven downriggers with good reason. He fishes right on the bottom in 100 to 300 feet of water. With inexperienced anglers, he is tending up to four lines almost by himself. He operates two downriggers and pulls the lines many times in a day of fishing. In addition to relieving the drudgery of pulling down riggers, while the motor is retrieving the line, he is working with other tackle.

Downriggers Avoid Floating Weeds

Normally, downriggers have little or no benefit when trolling shallow. However, if the water has floating weeds, downriggers can keep weeds off your lure. When trolling with a lure on monofilament line, floating weeds may get caught on your line, ride down the line to the lure and foul the lure. Even a wisp of weed on the lure kills its action and you don't catch fish.

With a downrigger, weeds are caught on the downrigger cable or the line both going almost straight down into the water. The line with the lure runs nearly straight back underwater and remains free of weeds.

Guide Chris Turner holds up a lake trout.

Downrigger Releases

The different downrigger releases have different advantages. Most downrigger releases are spring tension clips. You squeeze the line between two spring-loaded rubber pads. The amount of force required to pull the line free on other models can be adjusted to a light setting by barely catching the line in the edge of the rubber tension pads. It can be adjusted for a heavier release force by moving the line far back into the tension pads.

You want a light pull from a fish to release the clip so even a small hooked fish will pull the line from the downrigger. You want the clip to hold the line firmly enough to put some tension on the rig as it is lowered and you tighten the line to minimize slack line between the rod and clip. Set the clip for too much tension and a fish won't pull the line free when it is hooked; set it with insufficient tension and the line pops out easily from the water drag on the line or when lowering the downrigger.

With these friction clips, the vertical force applied by the rod will release the line just as easily as the horizontal pull of a hooked fish. I have been frustrated many times when I have set up the line, lowered the downrigger to depth and reeled line in to apply as much tension as I dared. Misjudging how much tension I could apply I pulled the line from the clip, then I had to reel in the line, pull the downrigger and start over.

To overcome this problem, some downrigger clips have innovative designs that can sustain high vertical force from the rod yet be released by the lower force from a fish. One such device called a Rigger Trigger has a clever way of allowing a large vertical force from the rod while a light horizontal force on the bait or lure releases the line. Here the line goes through the spring-loaded tension pads, then through a trigger and continues back to the bait or lure. When the fish pulls, the trigger is actuated, the tension pads open and the line is free. Penn and other manufacturers have other ways of accomplishing a similar objective.

Stacking Lines on Downriggers

More than one rod can be used off one downrigger though the practical limit is two rods. In this procedure you clip the line from one rod off the weight or off the cable near the weight, reel out a certain amount of cable, perhaps 10 feet. You then clip a second downrigger clip to the cable and attach the line from a second rod to this clip. Finally let the cable out to the depth you selected for the deep line and the second line will be 10 feet shallower.

Claude Davis stacks lures off downriggers but he does it all on one rod and one line. He clips a line and leader off the downrigger weight in a conventional manner but he adds a sliding leader that slides freely on the line between the end of the rod and the downrigger weight. The line makes an arc in the water between the end of the rod and the clip. The extra leader and lure rides up and down that line and stabilizes at the midpoint of the line, so it is about half as deep as the lure at the end of the line.

When a fish bites and gets hooked, it pulls the line from the downrigger clip; the leader slides to the end of the line and the fish is landed. He catches fish on both the lure at the end of the line and the lure on the sliding leader.

To set up this rig, thread the line through the eye of a swivel before tying the line to the lure. Tie the mid-depth leader to the other eye of this free sliding swivel. This leader can only be six or seven feet long because it ends up at the end of the line with the slider against the lure tied to the end of the line. You can only reel down to the slider clip and that means the full length of the leader is extending from the rod tip. The leader must be short enough to bring the fish close enough to net.

Slow Down

Many times you will want to troll slowly and sometimes that is slower than the minimum speed on your outboard motor. An electric trolling motor can be adjusted until the propeller is barely rotating and you can troll as slowly as you want. This is one of the very good reasons to have a trolling motor even if you move from place to place with an outboard motor.

Another method to slow down is with a metal trolling plate that attaches to the back of your outdrive. This plate extends horizontally when running so it has minimum water resistance and doesn't slow your boat. To troll with one model, you mechanically trip the trolling plate to a vertical position behind the propeller blocking part of the water flow. Another model is spring-loaded so the force of the water at high speed moves it to the horizontal (up) position. The spring pushes it down into trolling position behind the prop at lower speeds.

You can also use a water brake to slow the velocity. This is a fabric device tied to the boat and dropped in the water. It drags in the water and slows the boat speed just as a parachute slows the rate of descent for a person in air. It is useful in many situations—none more important than slowing the speed when drift-trolling where you have no power to control your velocity.

You can also drag buckets behind the boat or beside the boat to slow down. At River's Lodge in Rivers Inlet, British Columbia, the owner tied plastic buckets to cleats on the side of the boat. I forgot to take the buckets out of the water after I pulled my lines and pushed the throttle forward to go home. The bucket on my side bounced once then on the second bounce it swung over the rail and dumped a bucket full of cold water down the back of my neck. I've always remembered after that to dump the water out of the buckets and lift them into the boat before I quit trolling.

Another method to slow down is running the boat backwards with the motor in reverse. You are pushing water with the stern, and the boat goes slower. This is only practical on calm days. On rough days, water can splash in over the transom.

When to Fish With a Long Line

When fishing for salmon, you may be trolling as shallow as 15 feet and the bait on a short leader behind a downrigger is only 15 to 20 feet from the boat. On many days these fish seem to be attracted to the boat and a bait or lure very close to the boat is fine.

At other times, particularly on freshwater lakes or rivers, fish shy away from the boat. While trolling shallow in clear water in Shasta Lake, Gary Miralles found that 50 feet of line out behind the downrigger wasn't enough. He caught only a few trout until he lengthened the line behind his downrigger to 80 to 100 feet. Apparently the boat spooked the fish and they weren't calmed down enough to bite until he got greater separation between his boat and his lure. When trolling deep, 30 feet or more, he keeps the lure closer to the downrigger.

High-Speed Trolling

Normally high-speed trolling for fast game fish like sailfish, marlin and tuna is at or just under the surface. However, some anglers are trolling with downriggers to catch these fish. Now the downrigger is no longer straight down and the indicated depth (a measure of the amount of cable out) isn't even close.

Adjustments to get the lure to the desired depth was a lot of guessing but now results shown in Chapter 11 show the depth trolled for any speed up to 10 mph and with as much as 200 feet of cable out.

Boat Setup

The number one consideration in locating downriggers on a boat is positioning them so the downrigger cable is safely clear of the prop and other equipment. This sounds easy but I have learned from experience that you can set up downriggers well away from the prop and still get in trouble.

I was trolling for salmon on Larry Humpherys' boat in rough seas. We normally wouldn't have even launched our boat in these conditions but it was our final day on a trip and we wanted to fish one last morning. He had mounted downriggers on each side of his boat with their arms protruding out from the boat. The downrigger cables were about five feet from the prop on the outdrive. We had fished hundreds of hours with this setup and had never had a problem.

Sometime about midmorning we caught a wave sideways. The wave lifted us up, moved us over and dropped us down. In that process the downrigger cable went slack and the lateral motion of the boat set the outdrive down onto one slack cable. The cable caught on the prop and whizzed out from the downrigger pulley as it wrapped around the propeller. Humpherys immediately knew what had happened and shut down the engine. We lifted the outdrive, reached down with the gaff, caught the downrigger cable, cut it and brought the weight in hand over hand. The boat was tossing too much to try to get the cable out of the outdrive. We radioed a friend fishing nearby to help and he towed us back to the dock.

Position your downrigger so it has good separation from the motor and outdrive. Consider the rolling, bouncing and tossing of the boat and realize even well-placed downriggers, under severe sea conditions, may not be safe. If you are fishing in rough seas, be certain the downrigger cables will always clear the prop or don't use them.

Another Way to Use a Dodger

One good way to set up a downrigger is with a flasher or dodger attached directly to the weight—not on the line with the lure or bait. You clip your fishing line to the downrigger cable above the weight. When a fish strikes, it pulls the line from the clip but the flasher is still attached to the weight—not the line. This

way you don't fight the attractor when playing a fish.

Lower the weight into the water until the flasher is just submerged. Let out enough line that the bait or lure is four to six feet behind the flasher. Attach the line to the clip and let the combination down. Work slowly so you can keep the two lines separated.

Dodgers like these trolled in front of a bait or lure can help attract fish.

Black Boxes Attract Fish

Scientists have found that a positive electrical charge around the downrigger cable attracts many species of fish. Using an electronic gadget called the Black Box, you can set up your boat and downrigger to attract fish. The charge must be right for each species. Researchers have found and tabulated what charge is best for each species — you can dial in the optimum charge on the Black Box. This is a more advanced part of downrigger trolling and is covered in detail in Chapter 14.

Downriggers are a good way to meet many trolling challenges. They get the bait or lure to a

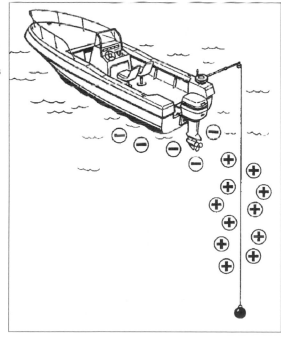

precise depth and can take it very deep. They can also keep a lure free of trash when a lake or river has floating debris.

CHAPTER 9

Know Your Depth

Thanks to technological advances, we can locate fish and know how deep we should be fishing. State-of-the-art fish finders can now read fish depth directly, or at least infer their location by zeroing in on schools of baitfish or analyzing bottom structure. We know what water temperature each species will seek and can measure this at various depths to pinpoint the zones where we will probably find fish.

So we know what depth to fish. But can we take advantage of this information? How do we get our lure or bait to the right level? Typically we attach a weight that seems appropriate, estimate how much line we should spool out and hope for the best. The line usually loops back far behind the boat and the depth trolled is no better than a wild guess.

Experienced trollers devise techniques that usually work for them. A friend uses a one-quarter-ounce weight on four-pound-test line and counts 10 times across the spool on the reel as the line zips back and forth, and he catches fish. He knows he is fishing about 10 feet deep because his lure gets hung up any time he goes over a shallow spot 10 feet or less. But to adapt to a different depth, he could guess and maybe get in the general ball park, but wouldn't really know how deep he was fishing.

Guide Barry Canavero determined his trolling depth for striped bass by finding a sandbar that was 10 feet deep, his desired trolling depth. With a line length counter on his reel, he trolled back and forth across that bar letting out line on each pass. When he let out 200 feet of line, his lure touched bottom. He knows with the same rigs and at his normal trolling speed, his lure is 10 feet deep when he lets out 200 feet of line.

Sometimes anglers—particularly salmon trollers—get their bait or lure to the proper depth with heavy weights. The line goes almost straight down eliminating most of the guess work concerning trolled depth. But heavy weights and light tackle don't mix and this sure takes a lot of the sport out of sport fishing. Downriggers get the lure or bait to a known depth at typical slow trolling speeds but are fairly expensive, add a complication to trolling, aren't practical on rental boats and are a hazard if they get caught on the bottom or in the prop. Many fishermen avoid the complications of downriggers by not using them.

A friend and I consistently attract rainbow trout at a nearby lake by trolling a small silver lure on a leader at the end of 90 feet of lead-core line. We had seen fish on our fish finder at about 20 feet deep and thought we were fishing about that depth. I had an ultra-light spinning outfit rigged and ready to use and was hoping for a chance to catch one of these fish on this very sensitive tackle. I attached a one-half-ounce rubber core twist sinker onto my four-pound-test line, tied on the small silver lure that had been my most effective fish catcher and spooled out about 100 feet of line.

After 20 minutes of fruitless fishing and not knowing my trolling depth, I considered changing back to lead-core line. Suddenly, my light rod bowed and jerked. The reel spun and a trout cleared the water behind the boat. Because I was using light tackle, the fish felt larger than my previous fish, but a few minutes later we scooped up a 14-inch rainbow typical of the fish we had been catching.

Convinced that I had stumbled onto the right combination, I hurried to get my line back in the water. I trolled with this ultra-light rig three-quarters of an hour but my earlier success was not repeated. Perhaps the fish were deeper. I ran out an additional 50 feet of line, but after another half-hour my companion had caught two more fish on his lead-core line rig while I was still looking for a hit. I gave up and went back to the proven setup.

Had I known how to troll at the right depth, I could have used the preferred ultralight tackle and taken fish. I thought back to an analysis I made to calculate trolling depth when taking partial differential equations in college and knew it was time to dust off this analysis and find the answer.

Scientific Depth Calculations

There is a way to know how deep you are trolling. I've written and solved the equations that determine trolled depth and have applied the results to most trolling situations. Graphs in this and the next two chapters of this book show your line profile underwater and how deep you are trolling with a lure or bait.

Forces that lift an airplane or a kite are the same forces that act in the water. The hydrodynamics of trolling is exactly the same as aerodynamics except one is in air, the other is in water. The density of water is about 1000 times greater than air so the forces at a given velocity are about 1000 times greater in water.

By analyzing the force on the lure, weight and line from the movement through the water, plus the force of gravity (the only two forces acting) I found the contour of the line in the water and exactly how deep the lure or bait is trolled. The concept is simple but the equations are involved and you need to know something about hydrodynamics to develop the equations. (A description of the analysis is in the appendix.)

Too Many Variables

The underwater profile of the line as it is trolled through the water is shown for a typical freshwater trolling condition in Graph 9-1. The trolling velocity is 2 mph using a one-ounce weight on 100 feet of four-pound-test line. Note how the line comes up steeply from the weight and flatten out near the surface. An important variable is speed and Graph 9-2 shows the line contour for the same parameters except the speed has been increased to 4 mph, twice the speed of the profile of Graph 9-1. Note how the weight and lure are much shallower— only 9.7 feet deep for 4 mph but 28.5 feet deep for 2 mph.

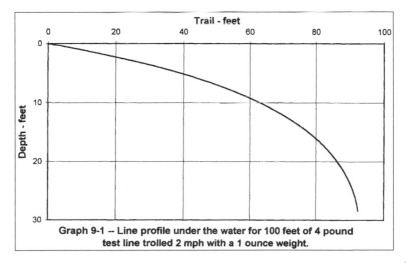

Graph 9-1 -- Line profile under the water for 100 feet of 4 pound test line trolled 2 mph with a 1 ounce weight.

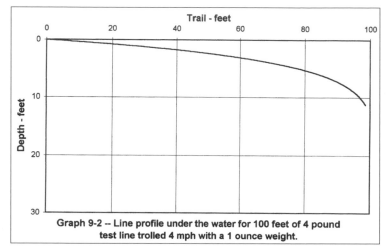

Graph 9-2 -- Line profile under the water for 100 feet of 4 pound test line trolled 4 mph with a 1 ounce weight.

Four factors influence depth trolled: (1) line diameter—which can also be thought of as line strength; (2) weight of the sinker or lure; (3) trolling speed; and (4) length of line below the water surface.

Four factors are too many to graph easily. We can plot the depth for one factor and we can understand two factors by putting in a number of curves on each graph. How do we evaluate so many variables? By using different graphs for different line strengths and making separate graphs for two line lengths, we can make a family of graphs to cover any fishing situation.

Table 1: LINE DIAMETER IN INCHES

Test Lb	Monofilament	Super line
2		
4	0.0076	
6	0.0094	0.0048
8	0.0110	
10	0.0120	0.0060
12	0.0132	
14	0.0143	
17	0.0164	
20	0.0180	0.0090
25	0.0200	0.0105
30	0.0220	
40	0.0255	
50	0.0285	0.0150
60	0.0315	
80	0.0360	

Velocity and Weight are Most Important

Two of the factors have a relatively small effect. The least important is line strength—at least within the line strengths used for a typical trolling situation. What really counts is the line diameter and typical line diameters (shown in Table 1) were found by measuring the diameter of lines from several manufacturers. Graph 9-3 shows the difference in trolled depth for two- to 20-pound-test line trolled with a two-ounce weight at one and 4 mph. Graph 9-4 shows similar curves for 20- to 80-pound-test line.

50

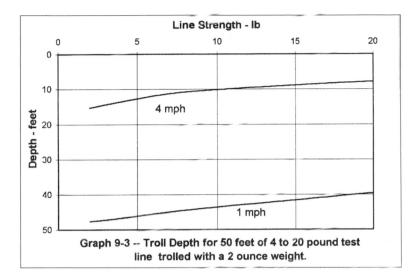

Graph 9-3 -- Troll Depth for 50 feet of 4 to 20 pound test line trolled with a 2 ounce weight.

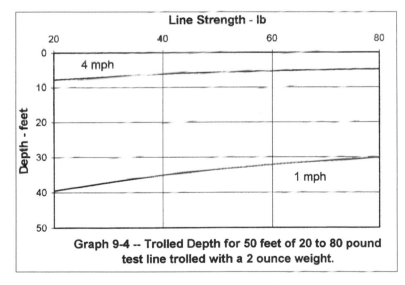

Graph 9-4 -- Trolled Depth for 50 feet of 20 to 80 pound test line trolled with a 2 ounce weight.

Note that these curves are very shallow, meaning depth changes are small for large changes in line strength. If, for example, we look at a narrow range of four- and six-pound-test line—typical for freshwater, light tackle trolling—the trolled depth is deeper for the lighter line, but not by much. Trolling with a two-ounce weight at 4 mph, 50 feet of six-pound-test line is trolled at a depth of 11.3 feet. Four-pound-test is trolled 12.8 feet deep. That is a difference of 1.5 feet or a little more than 10 percent for a line that is 50 percent stronger.

The point is whether you are trolling slow or fast, deep or shallow, the differences in trolling depth are small over a range of line strengths. The next two chapters have graphs for several different line strengths. Choose the graph for the line strength nearest the one you are using to find your trolling depth.

Length of Line Out

The second consideration, the length of line spooled out when the rig is trolled far behind the boat and the line is lying fairly flat on the surface, has a small effect. For example, with standard four-pound-test line and a two-ounce weight, 50 feet of line trolled at 3 mph will troll at a depth of 11.3 feet. Increasing the line out to 100 feet increases the depth to 14.1 feet. Even spooling out 200 feet of line only increases the depth to 17 feet. Sure these changes are significant but if you are in the fish catching zone with 100 feet of line out, you are probably still in the zone with less or more line out.

Of course if you are trolling with a heavy weight and the line goes almost straight down, a change in the length of line out makes a large change in trolling depth. If the line goes into the water at a steep angle, the depth is about the same as the length of line below the surface.

Graph for Each Range of Line Strength

In the next two chapters, different graphs are used for different types of fishing. Chapter 10 has graphs for fishing with a conventional line and a weight or a lure. Each graph was made for a specific line strength but the analysis can be applied to other similar strength lines with very little error. The line strengths are four-pound, 10-pound, 20-pound and 50-pound-test line. All are for conventional monofilament or Dacron line but they can be applied to super lines by adjusting the line strengths for each graph.

Trolling velocity and the weight of the sinker or lure are the two most important variables in determining trolled depth. Graph 9-5 relates depth fished to speed through the water trolling with 50 feet of four-pound-test line and a one-ounce weight. This graph shows that for a 4 mph trolling speed, the trolled depth is 7.8 feet. If the trolling speed is cut in half to 2 mph, the depth of the rig is more than doubled to 19.5 feet. Small changes in trolling speed make significant changes in trolled depth.

Graph 9-6 is the same as Graph 9-5 except curves for two additional weights

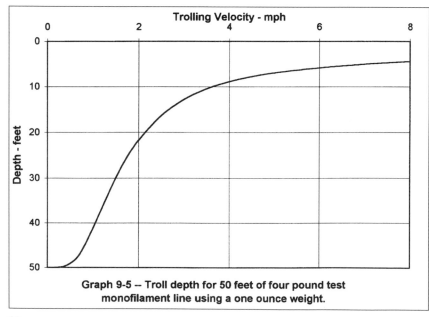

Graph 9-5 -- Troll depth for 50 feet of four pound test monofilament line using a one ounce weight.

have been added. (This is the type of graph that will be used in the next two chapters.) For one-quarter ounce of weight trolled at 2 mph, the trolled depth is 8.8 feet; for one ounce it is 21.7 feet and with four ounces, the depth is 39.9 feet. As you see, increasing or reducing the weight makes a large difference in trolled depth. Changing weights is a good way to change your trolling depth. Letting out more line or bringing in line may be used to make fine adjustments.

Velocity is Important

All of these calculations assume that we know our trolling speed. If a current is flowing in a river we must make our measurements relative to the water. Speed along a shoreline, even if we can measure it, is only part of the answer. Trolling velocity is an important factor, independent of depth so getting our bait to the right depth may not necessarily result in fish on the line. However, it is the first step toward improving our chances.

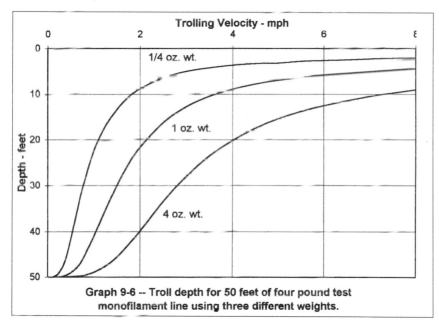

Graph 9-6 -- Troll depth for 50 feet of four pound test monofilament line using three different weights.

How do you know how fast your boat is moving through the water? If you have a good speedometer that will measure your low trolling speed accurately, you can read your velocity and choose how much weight you will use and how much line to let out. (See Chapter 12 for a review of speedometers and methods of finding your speed.)

On a recent salmon fishing trip I found that wind can affect trolled depth dramatically. We were trolling for salmon at the minimum throttle setting with about a 15 knot wind out of the south. We caught chinook salmon on shallow lines with four-ounce weights but we were only catching fish when heading south against the wind. As we were pushed by the wind on our northerly route, we didn't catch any fish.

We knew we were moving through the water faster and the trolled depth was shallower on the windward leg but we didn't know how much weight to add to get our bait to the right depth. Our speedometer said we were going about 2 mph against the wind and 3 mph going with the wind even at the lowest engine speed. How much difference would that velocity change make to our trolled depth? A four-ounce weight on 50 feet of 20-pound-test line trolled at 2 mph into the wind would take our rig down 29 feet on the productive leg at 2 mph (from Graph 10-5) but only 17 feet on the faster wind-aided return trip at 3 mph—probably enough difference to take us out of the fish zone. With this graph, we know that we need 10 ounces of weight on the wind-aided leg to get to the 29-foot depth we were trolling using a four-ounce weight against the wind.

This analysis assumes the water velocity is the same from the surface to the depth of the weight or lure. This may not be true for trolling in rivers, and sub-surface currents in the ocean or a large lake may also affect the depth. However, most of the time the depth shown on the graphs will be very close.

Use Low-drag Lures

These graphs apply directly to trolling with a weight, well behind the boat, using a lure or bait that has a low drag. Many lakes are crammed with small baitfish like minnows, threadfin shad and silversides and most game fish go for these baits or light, low-drag imitations of them. Small lures like Triple Teazers, Needlefish, Dick Nites, Mepps Spinners or Panther Martins imitate these baitfish and are trolled at the depth shown in these graphs. Lures like Kastmasters, Z-Rays and Cripplures are heavy and the weight of the lure is the weight to use when reading the graphs.

If the lure trolled behind a weight is heavy, it will run deeper than shown but if it is light and has a lot of drag, it will run more shallow. Use a slightly heavier weight or slower trolling speed to get high drag lures to the desired depth.

Get in the Zone

Fish are usually in a depth zone. One will be at 15 feet, the next one may be 18 feet deep and another one will be 14 feet deep. Not all fish are at the same depth so your goal is usually to get your lure into the fish zone, not to a precise depth. With these graphs, if you know your parameters, you can get accurately to your depth. If you don't know your velocity or other parameters exactly or lure drag makes your lure shallower, you can usually estimate and still get to the fish catching zone.

Trolled depth is one of the most important factors in catching fish but most people don't know how deep they are trolling. Armed with these graphs, a suit-able selection of weights and some form of trolling speedometer, you can master any trolling situation. Use them to find your trolled depth and see if your catch at the end of the day isn't greatly improved.

CHAPTER **10**

Basic Trolling Depth

The most basic trolling method is trolling with monofilament line with a lure or bait, with or without a weight. The graphs in this chapter show your trolled depth for trolling with this configuration. You can set up your line and sinker weight to get the desired trolled depth for conventional monofilament line, Dacron line and super lines like Fireline or Spiderwire. Graphs in this chapter are for four different line strengths from four-pound to 50-pound line strength and for trolling with 50 feet and 100 feet of line.

Each set of graphs is made for a specific line strength but the analysis can be applied to other similar strength lines with very little error. The line strengths are for light freshwater fishing (4-pound-test monofilament line); medium freshwater or light saltwater fishing (10-pound test line); heavy freshwater and medium saltwater (20-pound-test line); and heavy saltwater (50-pound-test line). Note these results are for monofilament line but are very close for Dacron line. The important factor is the diameter of the line and super lines like Fireline and Spiderwire need to be adjusted as follows. For 10-pound super line use the 4-pound monofilament curve; for 25-pound super line, use the 10-pound monofilament curve and for 50-pound super line, use the 20-pound-test monofilament curve.

Each graph has three weights that are chosen to include a typical range of weights that may be used with that strength line. A light weight is chosen; a medium weight is four times as heavy as the light weight and a heavy weight is four times as heavy as the medium weight. That makes the heavy weight 16 times as heavy as the light weight which covers all but the most unusual trolling situations.

If you want to troll with a really light weight, say a one-quarter-ounce weight on 10-pound-test line, (a one-half-ounce weight is the lightest shown for this weight line) assume you will troll half as deep as shown on the one-half-ounce curve. If you want to troll with a weight heavier than shown on the graph, you can estimate the trolled depth and probably be very close.

A large number of graphs are shown to cover all of the different trolling conditions but don't let the number of graphs intimidate you. Once you have decided what line strength you will use and how much line you will let out, you can go to that graph and ignore the other graphs.

Two Graphs for Each Line Strength

Two graphs are shown for each line strength. The first is trolling with 50 feet of line and the second is trolling with 100 feet of line. This is 50 or 100 feet of line in the water—not from the tip of your rod.

Graphs 10-1 and 10-2 show the depth trolled for four-pound-test line. Trolling depth is not very sensitive to line strength so any conventional monofilament line with a strength of two- to six- and even eight-pound-test strength can be used with only small errors. Super lines like Fireline and Spiderwire are much smaller in diameter and this curve is correct for 10-pound-test super lines.

If the lure or bait is small and adds only a little drag, the depth shown will be very accurate. If the lure is heavy, add the weight of the lure and sinker and use the combined weight when using the graph. If you aren't using a sinker, use the weight of the lure to determine your depth. If the terminal gear adds a lot of drag, the rig will ride up higher than calculated. In most cases, the difference in depth will be small and your lure or bait will still be in a good fish-catching zone.

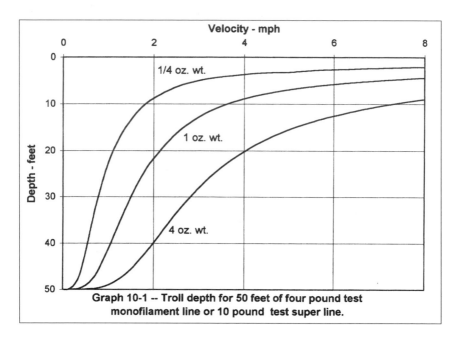

Graph 10-1 -- Troll depth for 50 feet of four pound test
monofilament line or 10 pound test super line.

How to Use the Graphs

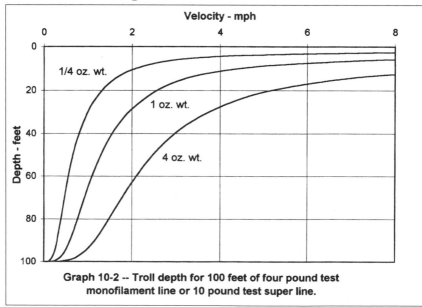

Graph 10-2 -- Troll depth for 100 feet of four pound test
monofilament line or 10 pound test super line.

How do you use these graphs? I'll run through some examples. Your depth finder shows fish at a depth of 15 feet. If you are trolling a one-ounce lure on 50 feet of four-pound-test line, how fast should you troll to get to these fish? Turn to Graph 10-1, starting at 15 feet on the depth scale on the left. Move horizontally across the graph, until you come to the one-ounce weight curve. Move straight up to the velocity scale above and read the trolling speed. The answer is to troll a little faster than 2 1/2 mph so adjust your speed to that velocity.

You probably have a standard trolling speed so here are the steps to troll a lure at a specific depth for a given velocity. (1) Decide what line strength you will be using. For the best accuracy use the exact line strength of line shown in the graph. For trolling for trout choose four-pound line. (2) Decide how much line you will let out. Select 50 feet or 100 feet so you can use one of the two graphs directly. (3) Go to the graph for the line strength and the length of line you selected (4) Find the velocity on the horizontal scale and draw or visualize a vertical line at that velocity. (5) Find the depth you want to troll on the vertical axis and draw or visualize a horizontal line from this point. (6) The weight you need to use is where these two lines cross. If they cross on or very near a weight curve, that is the weight. If it is between curves, choose a weight between the ones on the curves.

For example, if you are trolling at 2 mph with four-pound-test line, plan to run out 50 feet of line and want to get to fish you see on your fish finder at a depth of 20 feet, look at Graph 10-1. With a one ounce weight you will be trolling at a depth of 22 feet. So put on one ounce of weight and let out 50 feet of line and you will be at the desired depth. You may be trolling a bit deeper than you want and you can adjust the weight slightly or let out a bit less line. However, lure drag will tend to lift the rig slightly and you will be very close to your trolled depth of 20 feet without any adjustment. If you want to troll farther behind the boat, go to Graph 10-2, note that you need three-quarter ounces of weight to troll 20 feet deep. Put on a one half and a one-quarter-ounce weight and let out 100 feet of line.

If you want to get your lure halfway between the two depths of adjacent curves, what weight do you choose? If you are trolling at 2 mph, you will notice the depth with 50 feet of four-pound-test line out is 9 feet for the 1/4-ounce weight (actually 8.76 feet) and 22 feet for the one ounce weight (actually 21.7 feet). How do you get your lure halfway between these two or to a depth of 15.5 feet? The weight should be about halfway between these two weights (one-half of 1/4 plus one ounce) or 5/8 of an ounce.

Use and Limitation

You can apply these graphs to trolling with bait or a light lure with weights. Or you can apply them to heavy lures but recognize large, heavy lures probably have significant drag and will troll slightly shallower than shown in these graphs. Since fish attack from below, noting the fish's depth and setting up for that depth will put your lure slightly shallower, probably at a good fishing depth.

Diving lures like crankbaits are different. They dive and apply extra forces to a weight so these graphs can give you a guide for fishing diving lures behind a weight but the amount of dive and drag from the lure is a large factor and you must take these into account when using these graphs. If you err, try to keep your lure or bait above the fish.

You need to know your trolling velocity to use these graphs accurately. If you have a good trolling speedometer, read your velocity directly. If you don't know, estimate your velocity. As you make checks against these graphs, you can use them to determine your velocity for a given motor setting. Your trolled depth may not be accurate if you have made a poor initial velocity estimate but you will soon learn how fast you are trolling as we will discuss later.

Heavier Line

Graph 10-3 is for trolling with 50 feet of 10-pound-test monofilament line. The typical weights are a bit heavier so the curves are for one-half, two and eight ounces of weight. Graph 10-4 is for the same line except with 100 feet of line out. These curves also apply to 25-pound super line.

Graph 10-5 and 10-6 are for trolling with 20-pound-test monofilament line. This is for medium freshwater fishing or light saltwater fishing. The typical weights are heavier so the curves are for two, eight and 32 ounces of weight. The diameter of

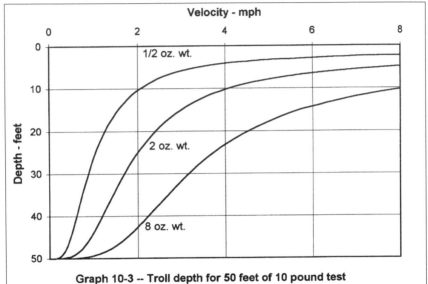

Graph 10-3 -- Troll depth for 50 feet of 10 pound test monofilament line or 25 pound test super line.

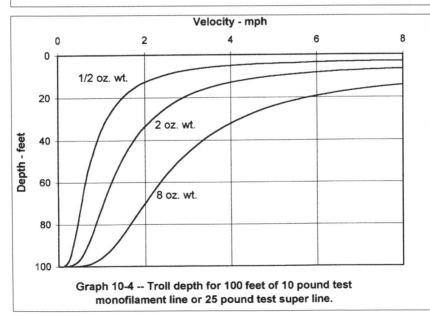

Graph 10-4 -- Troll depth for 100 feet of 10 pound test monofilament line or 25 pound test super line.

50-pound-test super line like Fireline or Spiderwire is the same as 20-pound-test monofilament so these curves also apply for 50-pound super line.
Graph 10-7 and 10-8 are for trolling with 50-pound-test monofilament line. The weight range is from two ounces to two-pounds. While these curves are for 50-pound-test monofilament, they can be used with very little error for 30-pound to 100-pound-test line. These eight graphs (Graphs 10-1 to 10-8) cover almost all fishing situations.

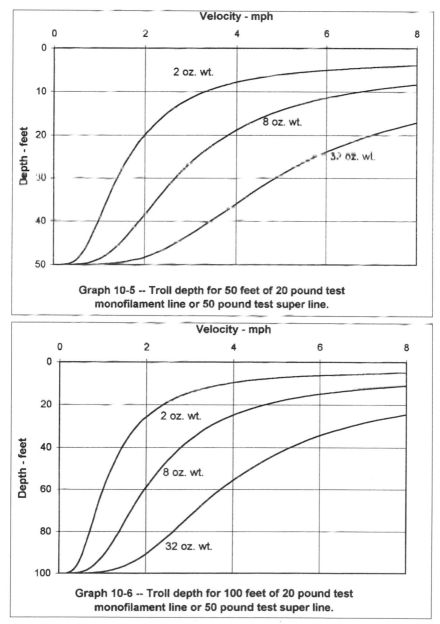

Graph 10-5 -- Troll depth for 50 feet of 20 pound test monofilament line or 50 pound test super line.

Graph 10-6 -- Troll depth for 100 feet of 20 pound test monofilament line or 50 pound test super line.

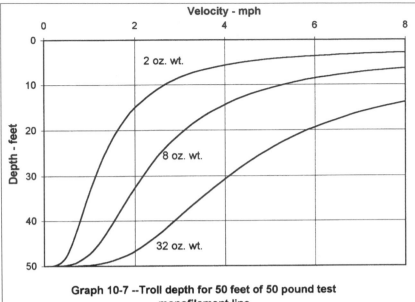

Graph 10-7 --Troll depth for 50 feet of 50 pound test monofilament line

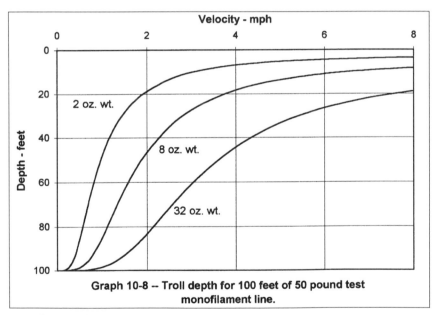

Graph 10-8 -- Troll depth for 100 feet of 50 pound test monofilament line.

Proof of Analysis

The results were checked in two ways. First I used my depth finder to measure the depth and let out enough line to hit bottom or just clear the bottom. The weight dragged bottom when the calculations said it would and cleared the bottom when the calculations showed it should clear confirming the depth analysis was correct.

In the second test I measured the contour of the line. I measured the angle of the line as it entered the water and compared the angle with the calculated angle. The line was lowered into the water and the angle measured at several pre-marked locations on the line and compared with the analysis. The agreement was very accurate showing that the line profile calculations were accurate. Knowing the line profile is correct is another confirmation that all of the calculations are accurate and the depth analysis is accurate.

Calibrate Your Speedometer as You Troll

If you always seem to be trolling shallower (or deeper) than shown, you should evaluate your line diameter, length of line out and amount of weight to be certain you are setting up according to the graph. Speedometers are notoriously inaccurate at slow speed so, if other factors are all correct, your velocity measurement is not accurate and needs to be corrected. If you are always deeper than you expect, you are trolling more slowly than you think; if you are trolling shallower, you are going faster than indicated.

If you think that at idle speed you are trolling two miles per hour, your depth with 50 feet of 10-pound-test line out with a half-ounce weight is 11 feet. If you drag bottom that is 14 feet deep, you must be going 1.7 mph or slower—Graph 10-3 shows your trolled depth for that weight and line is 14 feet. Draw a vertical line at 1.7 mph (or whatever velocity you are trolling) on the graphs you use and use this line on the graph to find the weight required when you troll at idle speed.

Once you know your speed, you can adjust to any new depth by adjusting weights or amount of line out to get to the desired depth. If you say you want to fish 30 feet deep another time, you know from the graphs at 1.7 mph, you need to use two ounces of weight with that same 10-pound-test line and to let out 50 feet of line. You can also use other line strengths, downriggers or weighted lines and know you can find your troll depth by using the 1.7 mph speed on these graphs.

Slow Trolling

The previous curves covered the velocity range of zero to eight mph. In most cases you can get parameters as accurately as you need from these graphs. Two

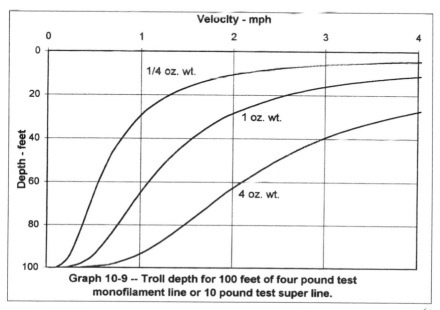

Graph 10-9 -- Troll depth for 100 feet of four pound test
monofilament line or 10 pound test super line.

additional graphs for a velocity range of zero to 4 mph are shown to help when you are trolling slowly. Graph 10-9 is for 100 feet of four-pound-test and Graph 10-10 is for 100 feet of 20-pound-test line.

Some ocean trolling conditions demand a long line. Graph 10-11 shows the underwater line profile for 200 feet of 20-pound-test line (a typical line strength used in the ocean or in saltwater estuaries) trolled 2 mph with a two-ounce weight.

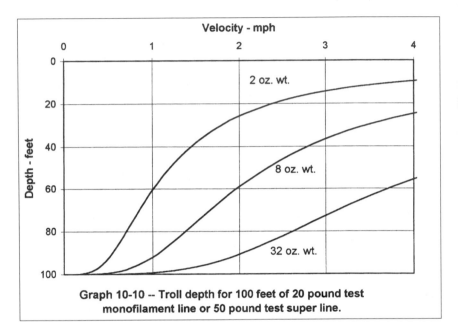

Graph 10-10 -- Troll depth for 100 feet of 20 pound test monofilament line or 50 pound test super line.

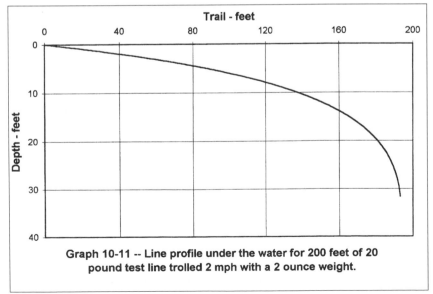

Graph 10-11 -- Line profile under the water for 200 feet of 20 pound test line trolled 2 mph with a 2 ounce weight.

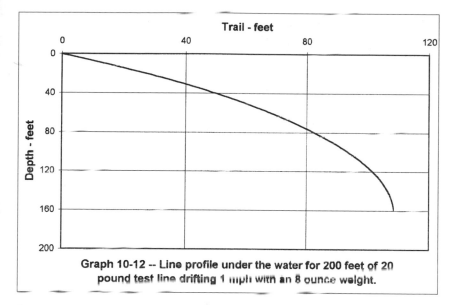

Graph 10-12 -- Line profile under the water for 200 feet of 20 pound test line drifting 1 mph with an 8 ounce weight.

Drift-fishing like drift-mooching for salmon and other fish is trolling at a very slow speed. The underwater line profile for drifting through the water at a speed of 1 mph with 200 feet of 20-pound-test monofilament line is shown in Graph 10-12. This graph shows that even drifting can put a large bow in the line.

The lure or bait is 160 feet deep. Even for drifting, you may need to make adjustments to get to the proper depth. The trail of 108 feet shows why lines from one side of the boat get tangled with lines from the other side. The line profile is different enough with different line strengths, different depths and different weights that lines from one side of the boat often cross and sometimes tangle with lines from the other side. One mph is a fast drift so the trail behind the boat or to the side of the boat may be much less under ideal conditions.

Line Angle is Deceptive

Don't overcompensate to get deep. You may be trolling deeper than you think. I thought trolling for salmon with a four-ounce weight with 50 to 100 feet of line out was shallow. The line came out from the boat at a shallow angle so it looked like the bait wasn't very deep. Actually with a four ounce weight on 20-pound-test line the bait was almost 30 feet deep and with 100 feet of line out it was 43 feet deep. I thought this was our shallow line. But when we had our downriggers and lines with heavier weights set at 30 to 40 feet deep our so called "shallow line" was our deepest line.

Trolling with a weight and a light lure or bait on a line is a basic fishing method. Without these graphs, estimating your trolling depth involves a lot of guessing, but now you don't need to guess your depth. Use these graphs to *know* how deep you are trolling.

CHAPTER 11

Depth with Downriggers, Lead-Core or Steel Line

Dick Pool, owner of Scotty Downriggers, was very interested when I told him I had calculated trolled depth for fishing with a line and a weight. I was surprised when he said anglers trolling with downriggers sometimes didn't know how deep they were fishing. I thought downriggers took your lure almost straight down and you just read the depth off the dial that counts out feet. Pool said some anglers are trolling fast with downriggers, the line and downrigger cable are swept back, the weight is raised up and the depth shown on the counter isn't accurate.

I told Pool I thought I could change my calculation to find the depth when trolling with a downrigger but I would need to have my results checked. We agreed I would make the calculations and he would make the measurements.

Two lines (the downrigger cable and the fishing line) dragging through the water complicates the analysis. However, both the downrigger cable and the line are moving through the water at the same velocity and drag is applied to both in proportion to their diameter. Perhaps just adding the diameter of the downrigger cable to the diameter of the line would give an accurate calculation. I made that adjustment and expected the result to be the downrigger cable contour as it is trolled through the water.

As I made these calculations, I found that you often aren't trolling as deep as your downrigger indicates even at moderate speed. At 2 mph with 200 feet out on the counter with a typical downrigger you are only trolling 170 feet deep, a 15 percent error. The downrigger will get the bait or lure deep but not as deep as shown on the counter on the downrigger.

Proof of Analysis

Pool made the measurements to check my analysis by dropping his weight down to the water's surface then zeroing his depth indicator. Next he dropped the weight a foot deep into the water and, using a protractor taped to a level, measured the angle of the cable relative to the horizon. He let out another foot of line, made another measurement, made another at four feet, eight feet, 15 feet, 30 feet, 60 feet and 100 feet on his counter. The measurement had to match my calculation at every depth to verify its accuracy.

When I compared the angle measurements at 4 mph and at 3 mph, they matched my calculation at every depth. This confirmed my calculations but I had one more set of data to match. The measurements at 2 mph didn't check. Speedometers on boats are notoriously inaccurate at slow speeds so I started adjusting the velocity. At 1.87 mph, the angle at every depth checked. If the measurement at some depths had checked and others were in error, I would have been suspicious of my calculation. When they all checked, it showed the true trolling velocity was 1.87 miles per hour. Pool's speedometer was accurate at 3 and 4 mph but when it registered 2 mph he was actually traveling 1.87 mph.

64

This was about the best check I could make. It showed the depth calculation was accurate if the velocity was known. Once the calculation was verified at 3 and 4 mph, the analysis could even determine the trolled velocity from the measurements taken at lower velocities.

Line Profile

Graph 11-1 shows the profile of a typical downrigger with a 10-pound weight trolled 3 mph. With 200 feet on the counter the weight and lure or bait is only 143 feet deep. Even with 100 feet of cable out, the trolled depth is 84 feet, a significant deviation from the indicated depth. Results of calculations to relate the actual trolled depth to the depth shown on the downrigger are summarized in Graphs 11-2, -3 and -4. Use these graphs to determine your true trolling depth when using downriggers.

For these calculations, the downrigger cable has a strength of 125 pounds and is 0.032 inches in diameter. The line is 20-pound-test line with a diameter of 0.018 inches.

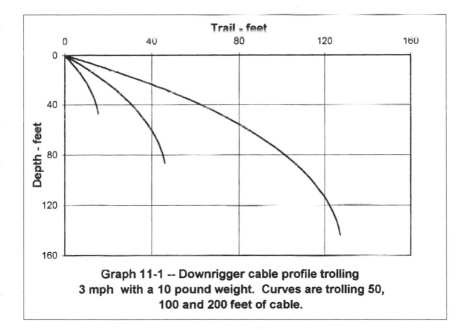

**Graph 11-1 -- Downrigger cable profile trolling
3 mph with a 10 pound weight. Curves are trolling 50,
100 and 200 feet of cable.**

As we saw when evaluating lines, changing the strength of the line and, in this case, the cable and the line, doesn't change the result very much. The 125-pound cable and 20-pound line in this example are typical for a middle range downrigger so only that combination has been analyzed. Most downriggers with 10-pound weights, even with a heavier line or a slight variation in cable, will troll the bait or lure very close to the depth shown. If you want to use these results very accurately, make certain your downrigger cable is about 0.032 inches in diameter and use line that is about 0.018 inches in diameter (20-pound-test monofilament line or 50-pound-test super line). Changes in line diameter for different strength lines are small so using line strengths from four to 40 pounds will have a small deviation.

Graph 11-2 shows the actual trolled depth for four different lengths of downrigger cable. To get to a desired trolling depth, find your velocity on Graph 11-2 and drop down to the trolled depth. If this point falls on one of the curves on the graph, let out cable until the counter shows that number. You won't usually be so lucky to be exactly on one of the curves but you can extrapolate between curves to accurately determine the setup. For example, if you want to troll 90 feet deep at 3 mph, you note that letting out 100 feet of cable gets you to 81 feet deep and 150 feet on the downrigger counter puts your lure at a true depth of 117 feet. Let out 115 if you want to be slightly on the shallow side of 90 feet or 120 feet if you want to be at least 90 feet deep. You may be two or three feet in error but you are usually looking for a depth zone, and that will put you well within that zone.

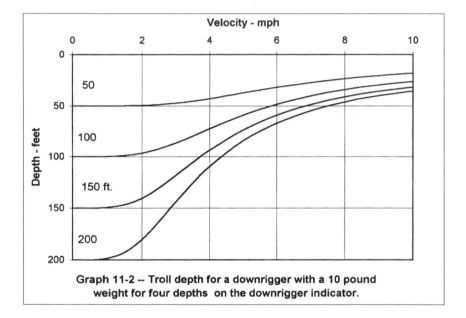

Graph 11-2 -- Troll depth for a downrigger with a 10 pound weight for four depths on the downrigger indicator.

Graphing Your Depth

The weight used with the downrigger is important. Most sports downriggers have weights of seven to 15 pounds so that is the range of weights for this analysis. Graph 11-3 shows the trolled depth for the same line and cable with a seven-pound downrigger weight and Graph 11-4 shows the trolled depth for a 15-pound downrigger weight. These three curves bracket most downrigger trolling setups.

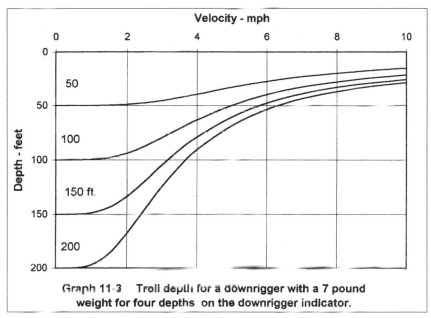

Graph 11-3   Troll depth for a downrigger with a 7 pound weight for four depths on the downrigger indicator.

For all three of these weights, the depth shown on the downrigger is your true trolling depth for up to 200 feet deep and 1 mph or slower. Between 1 and 2 mph, the errors build and are as great as 15 percent at 2 mph. When the velocity is 4 mph, the depth of the lure with the lighter weight may be less than half as deep as the downrigger indicates and it may be about half as deep as indicated with the 10-pound weight. Errors from the indicated depth continue to increase as the velocity increases.

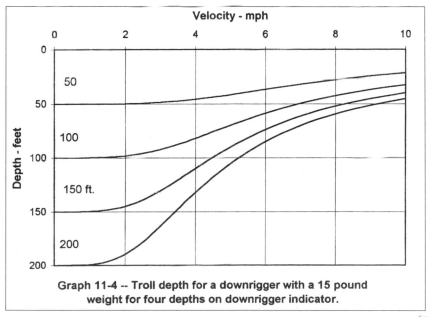

Graph 11-4 -- Troll depth for a downrigger with a 15 pound weight for four depths on downrigger indicator.

Of course the largest deviations are with the greatest amount of cable out. These results show that even at modest trolling speeds, the deviation from the indicated depth is significant and these graphs should be used when you are trolling deep and faster than 1 mph. When 50 feet or less are shown on the counter, the indicated troll depth is accurate to 2 to 3 mph.

A downrigger is the most accurate method to get your lure or bait to the desired depth. The heavy weight overpowers forces from lures and your downrigger weight will be at the depth on the graph. If you troll with a short leader, your lure or bait will be at the same depth as the weight. If you let out a lot of line behind the downrigger, a diving lure or heavy lure will go deeper than the weight. A light lure or bait will be the same depth as the downrigger weight even on a long leader.

Lead-core Line Characteristics

Another method to get deep is to troll with a weighted line. Lead-core line and steel line are the two common weighted lines. The configurations of these lines and the line and leader setup are discussed in Chapter 7.

With weighted lines, the angle of the line through the water is constant from the surface to the leader. If your lure is at a depth of five feet when you spool out ten yards of line, with 20 yards of line your lure will be 10 feet deep; with 30 yards of line it is 15 feet deep and with 100 yards of line out it is 50 feet deep.

One hundred yards of typical 15-pound-test strength lead-core line weighs about 5.2 ounces. The line diameter is 0.025 inches and the lead core is 0.016 inch diameter. Each 10 yards of each color weighs 0.52 ounces. With two colors out, the weight in the water is 1.04 ounces. Lead-core lines from different manufacturers are not the same and will troll at different depths. When I compared Gudebrod, Sunset and Cabela's lead-core lines of 13, 15 and 18 pounds, the first two had about the same weight to diameter ratio but the Cabela's lines were a little heavier for a given weight so would troll a bit deeper. Because of these differences, the troll depth of lead-core line from different manufacturers or of different strengths will not be exact. They will be close for most lead-core lines of all strengths and the graphs are good starting points for trolling with this line.

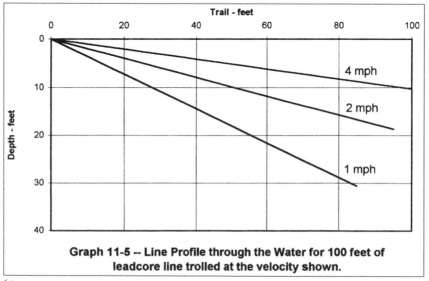

Graph 11-5 -- Line Profile through the Water for 100 feet of leadcore line trolled at the velocity shown.

Graph 11-5 shows the profile of lead-core line with 100 feet of line out at 1, 2 and 4 mph. Remember weighted lines go into the water at an angle and maintain that angle at all depths. If you double the amount of line in the water you will double your trolling depth.

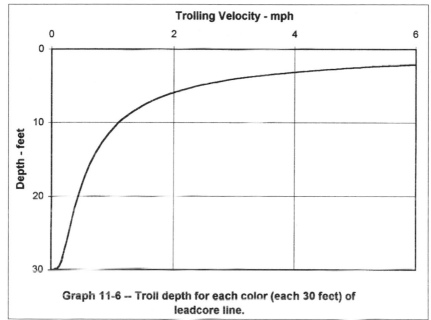

Graph 11-6 -- Troll depth for each color (each 30 feet) of leadcore line.

Graph 11-6 shows how deep you are trolling for each color of line in the water (remember, a color is 30 feet) for a range of velocities. To determine your trolling depth, find your velocity on the graph then find the corresponding depth. This is the depth if you let out one color (30 feet) of line. To find the trolled depth multiply this number by the number of colors in the water.

For example, if you are trolling at 2 mph your depth is 5.7 feet for each color of lead-core. With three colors of lead-core out you multiple that number by three and find you are trolling 17.1 feet deep.

Since different weight lead-core lines don't all troll at the same depth you may need to adjust for your line. If you find you are dragging bottom at depths where you expect to clear the bottom, or clearing the bottom when you should be dragging bottom, your trolling velocity isn't exactly right or your lead-core line may be heavier or lighter than the typical line used for the calculations. The graph will usually be close enough to be in a good fish catching zone but you can find an accurate value for the depth trolled. Divide your actual trolled depth by the number of colors. As before, multiply this depth by the number of colors of lead-core line in the water to find your trolling depth.

Steel Lines
The depth trolled for each 100 feet of steel line is shown in Graphs 11-7 and 11-8. Results for a solid steel line shown in Graph 11-7 are slightly deeper than for the multistrand line shown in Graph 11-8. The multistrand line includes voids so it is larger in diameter for a given strength and weight. The solid steel line is 0.015 inch in diameter and the multistrand line is 0.020 inch in diameter. These lines both have a strength of about 40 pounds.

Use these graphs just as in the case of the lead-core line by multiplying the depth shown in the graph by the number of 100-foot lengths of line you have played out. At a speed of 2 mph, the solid line trolls at a depth of 19.4 feet for each 100 feet played out, and the multistrand line goes 17.8 feet deep for each 100 feet in the water.

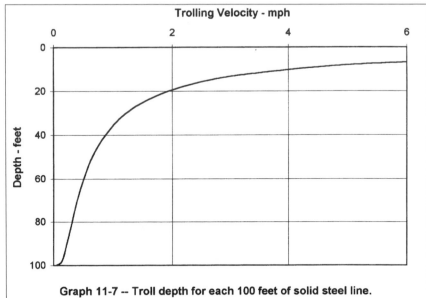

Graph 11-7 -- Troll depth for each 100 feet of solid steel line. Line is 0.015 inch in diameter.

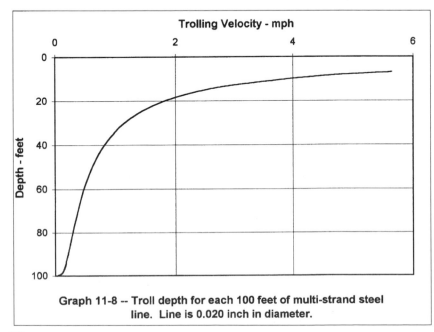

Graph 11-8 -- Troll depth for each 100 feet of multi-strand steel line. Line is 0.020 inch in diameter.

Low-Stretch Lines

Weighted lines have another advantage—they are low-stretch lines. The amount of stretch in a line is proportional to the length of the line so fishing with long lines normally means a lot of stretch. Steel has very little stretch and the sheath for the lead-core line is usually Dacron, also a low-stretch material, so these lines are sensitive and fish well even with long lines.

As with trolling with a weight, these calculations do not account for the dive or drag of lures. Diving or heavy lures will troll deeper and light lures with a lot of drag will troll shallower. These graphs work best with light lures that have little drag.

Wrap-up

The best way to use all of these graphs is to carry them with you on the boat and apply them on the spot. To troll your lure or bait at a particular depth, go to the appropriate graph to find how much weight you need, what length of weighted line or how much downrigger cable to spool out to get to a particular depth.

CHAPTER **12**

Boat and Tackle

A boat for trolling in freshwater can be as small as a canoe, a car-top boat, a folding or inflatable boat or as large as a cruiser for ocean fishing. The first consideration is safety so the boat must be large and seaworthy enough to handle all water and weather conditions you might encounter. A small boat that is great for small, protected lakes and placid rivers isn't safe on a larger lake or the ocean. Have a very seaworthy craft for fishing on the ocean or large lakes where waves can build quickly and fog can settle in reducing visibility to almost zero.

My idea of a perfect boat for most freshwater trolling is a 14- or 15-foot long aluminum boat with a 10 to 25 horsepower outboard motor. I like console steering but that is a luxury. An outboard motor can be used as a trolling motor but I like to troll with an electric motor—I can really feel the peace and quiet and hear the call of birds and the honking of geese. An inexpensive electric motor lets you troll at the very slow speed required for some lures.

For small lakes, you don't even need a conventional outboard motor—an electric trolling motor is perfect. Many small urban lakes permit only electric motors. Even a motor isn't essential—rowing is a very effective trolling method. The little surge you give the lure every time you make a stroke on the oars gives it an extra rhythmic action and is a great enticer of fish. But unless you are really in good shape or want to use this as a conditioning or body building exercise, you are going to wear out before you have trolled very long and you will probably decide you need a motor of some sort.

If you want to fish in shallow rivers, you need a sturdy flat-bottom boat often referred to as a sled. You may need a water jet drive on your outboard motor to go over the shallow areas.

Saltwater Fishing Boat

The primary requirement for a saltwater trolling boat is safety. You want a boat large enough and seaworthy enough to handle any sea conditions you might encounter. For fishing on the ocean, I like to have a lot of freeboard above the surface of the water. I also want an enclosed cabin where, if I get caught in rough seas, the water goes over the top of the cabin and not into the boat.

The boat must have either Global Positions System (GPS) or LORAN. If you already own LORAN and it functions well where you fish, it is probably okay. But LORAN is being phased out and the prices of GPS units are coming down rapidly. Small, accurate hand-held units cost less than $100. One of these navigational aids is essential for safety and can be used to return to fish or to set up a trolling pattern.

Speedometer

Velocity is one of the most important parameters in using the graphs in this book to determine trolled depth. A good speedometer that is accurate at a slow trolling speed will show your speed through the water, the parameter you need to set up the proper depth and get good bait or lure action.

Low priced speedometers measure water pressure in a tube pointed in the direction of travel—called a pitot tube. The pressure is proportional to the

An array of rods troll for salmon off a private boat

velocity squared so when you cut your velocity in half, you quarter the pressure you are sensing. Speed is related to pressure and the readout is in miles per hour or knots. (Multiply knots by 1.15 to get mph) This type speedometer works well at about 5 mph and faster, but at low velocities the pressure is too low to sense so the indicator doesn't even move off its peg.

More expensive speedometers operate off impeller wheels that turn at about the rate of travel through the water. These work well down to a couple of mph and may make a measurement at about 1 mph but are not very accurate at the lowest speeds. The better ones have two ranges, one for trolling and one for cruising speeds.

Use this speedometer but note deviations. If you consistently hang your lure when the graphs say you should clear a shallow spot or if you never touch the bottom where the graphs say you should, adjust your speed.

An alternative type speedometer that will accurately show your trolling speed mounts to the side or stern of your boat and drags a weight in the water. An arrow on a pivot points to your correct speed. Luhr-Jensen makes one called Luhr-Speed Trolling Speed Indicator. These are accurate and inexpensive but are a bit cumbersome.

Perhaps the ultimate in speedometers is a model that attaches to your downrigger weight and is lowered with the downrigger. An electrical cable runs up the downrigger cable

A simple and inexpensive Luhr-Speed accurately measures slow trolling speeds.

and is attached to the instrument in the boat. It reads both speed and temperature. Underwater currents can make the lure velocity different from the surface velocity. With this device you know what is happening at the lure. You know precisely how fast your lure is being trolled and can adjust your speed if it is different from the surface velocity.

With this device you can read the temperature as you lower your downrigger, find the thermocline, stop in or just above the thermocline and know your lure is precisely where the fish are. What is the drawback of this unit? It is a bit pricey at about $400 even at tackle discount mail order houses.

Other Ways of Knowing Trolling Speed

If you have a very basic boat without a speedometer, you may calibrate your speed by trolling alongside another boat that has an accurate speedometer. Or buy or borrow a Luhr-Speed indicator to calibrate your speed even if you find it too cumbersome to use all of the time.

If you have an electric motor, make a table of your speed versus your troll speed setting but be aware your speed slows as your battery discharges. Calibrate your speed for different throttle positions on your outboard motor. Determine your speed at the lowest throttle position and at your normal trolling speed. If you have a tachometer, write down your speed for different engine RPMs.

If you don't have a speedometer you can use the graphs in Chapter 10 to find your trolling velocity. On a day with little or no wind to influence your boat speed on a lake (so you have no current) let line out or add weight until you drag the bottom then relate that to the velocity in the graphs. For example, if at your normal trolling speed with a one-ounce weight you must let out 50 feet of four-pound-test line to touch a 22-foot-deep bottom, you know from the graph for these conditions that you are traveling 2 mph.

After you have trolled a while and relate your velocity to when you drag or clear the bottom, you will know your true velocity for your trolling speed. Winds are an important factor. At trolling speeds, the effect of wind on your boat can slow or speed your boat significantly. Don't try to calibrate your trolling speed on a windy day, wait for a calm day. Your throttle setting may need to be changed dramatically to get the desired trolling speed when the wind is blowing.

Troll at a Precise Depth

To get the best accuracy from the graphs in this book, set up precisely as indicated in the graph. Use the line strength and the line lengths shown. Use light lures that don't have much drag and the graph will be accurate. A lure with a lot of drag applies extra force not accounted for in the calculation so it trolls more shallow than shown in the graphs.

Mark your line at 50 and 100 feet so you can let out exactly that amount of line. Marks on your line will wear off after a few fishing trips. When they come off you can continue to keep track of how much line you have out by knowing how many times across the reel the line goes with a level wind reel to get to 50 or 100 feet. Count the number of transits while the marks are fresh on your line. After the marks are gone, you can count transits across the reel to get the desired length of line out.

Fish Finder

A fish finder is basic to finding fish either by seeing their representation on the screen, finding bait or by following bottom contours. Often you can see the fish or bait on the finder and know what depth to troll. At other times you are looking for bottom features that key where fish will be located. Fish travel in underwater channels like old riverbeds and a fish finder can help locate these routes. Or look for drop-offs where fish are likely to be waiting for food. Watch the depth on your fish finder and adjust your lure depth as you come to a shallow area so you don't snag all of your lures on the bottom.

If you have a battery in your boat, you can connect your finder off the battery. If you don't have a battery, look for fish finders that operate off their own internal batteries.

Spread Your Lures

Normal trolling runs your lure or bait in a narrow array behind the boat. You can have a rod extending out to spread your lines five or six feet on each side of the boat but the width of the trolling array is limited. Outriggers that extend out from the side of the boat spread lines farther but few sports anglers go to the expense or complication of having outriggers.

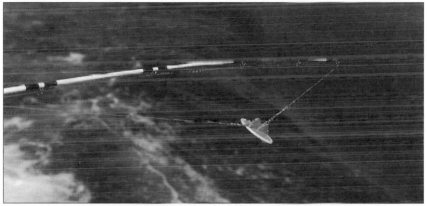

Divers like this one can be used to troll a lure or bait to depth.

Another approach is to use side planers. These float in the water and take an angle with the water—like an airplane flying sideways. To use one, play out the length of line you would fish behind the boat then attach the line to the side planer and let out more line to move the planer to the side of the boat.

This isn't just widening the array a little—one manufacturer claims his side planers can troll a bait or lure 150 feet to the side of the boat though I doubt anyone would troll so far to the side.

In congested areas you normally don't have space for wide-spread side planers—other boats would run over them. Use them when the lake or river is not crowded. When you fish a wide swath with your lure or bait away from the boat, fish that are boat shy will not be disturbed and may bite lures that are well away from the boat.

Tackle

The most important part of your tackle for freshwater trolling is a reel with a good drag. Spinning reels are good for light tackle fishing for small fish but for larger fish, you want the better drag capability and the forgiveness of a conventional revolving spool reel. Spinning reels are terrible line twisters when an angler reels without taking in line. Some reels have a six to one retrieve ratio. For every turn on the reel handle, the take-up bail turns six complete revolutions—the line is twisted six revolutions for each turn of the reel handle. It doesn't take long to get hundreds of turns of twist in the line. Conventional reels don't twist the line—a major advantage.

A rod and reel are held by a strap off the rail while trolling at high speed.

Abu Garcia Ambassador, Shimano Calcutta or similar reels are ideal for freshwater fishing. Choose a model that will hold sufficient line. Most will hold plenty of monofilament line but select a large reel if you are using lead-core line.

The rod can be an inexpensive graphite rod for trolling in freshwater. It is used primarily to play the fish so the most important feature is its flexibility. The rod should have a good bend when you have the drag on your reel set properly but have adequate strength to apply force to a fish. A six-foot six-inch rod for six- to 14-pound line is good for trolling for trout and most freshwater fish. For salmon in rivers or large salmon in lakes, a stronger rig is in order. A rod for 10- to 25-pound line is about right for these larger fish.

Ocean trolling rods are generally made from fiberglass because it makes heavier, tougher rods. Rods range from light rods to troll for small fish to rods designed for 100-pound line or more to troll for tuna, sailfish, marlin, wahoo and other large saltwater fish.

When to Change Line

Monofilament line ages well if it isn't exposed to ultraviolet lights (fluorescent lights or sunlight) or certain chemicals. It can last for years but it is one of the cheaper pieces of equipment and should be changed regularly just on general principle. Nicks and cuts near the end of the line can really weaken the line so cut off the end of the line frequently. A large fish applies extra force that puts added strain on the line and is likely to break free. Don't risk losing a big fish by saving a few dollars fishing with old line. Don't even think about fishing with line that is chalky colored. This line is way beyond its useful life and will break easily.

Lead-core line is usually much stronger than the leader so it can be degraded and still the line will be stronger than the leader. I'm not certain this is good practice but I have used lead-core line for several years. A bigger concern is that the colors fade so I have difficulty telling how many colors of line I am trolling.

Most of the equipment discussed here can be found in boat and fishing catalogs like Bass Pro Shop (1935 S. Campbell, Springfield, MO 65898) and Cabela's (812 - 13 Ave., Sidney, NB 69160). Write them to get free catalogs. These are good for standard items and are great references, but sometimes you want to see what you are buying or discuss pros and cons of equipment with a qualified distributor. That's the time to buy from your local tackle shop.

CHAPTER **13**

Reading the Water

When you decide to fish a body of water, you usually have a wide range of choices of where and how deep to fish. Do you fish the shallows along the shore or go to the deepest hole in the river or deepest part of the lake? Do you troll deep or shallow? Trolling covers a lot of area but you still need to know what kind of water to fish and have a plan. Choosing where to fish is the first decision in catching fish.

The amount of planning is largely a personal matter. Some people want to get really organized and do everything to maximize their success. They probably have a game plan as to where and how they will fish hour by hour during the day. Tournament anglers must take planning and organization to the extreme to be successful.

Others approach fishing as a diversion and say they must be organized on their job. Part of the fun of fishing for them is that they can be spontaneous and avoid all but essential planning. If getting too organized takes the fun out of fishing for you, don't do it. Just get your basic equipment together and go fish. Ask a few questions at the marina and go for it.

Choosing the Best Waters to Fish

You have a choice of lakes, rivers or ports. If you want to maximize your chance to catch fish, do your homework to decide which water is producing the best catch. Read reports from newspapers; go to a website for the latest information or call marinas and ask for fishing reports.

If you have fished a lake or river frequently, you know exactly where and how you will fish. You know what time you will launch your boat or when to get to the marina to rent a boat. You know where to start fishing, how deep to troll, what lures to use and have alternate fishing locations if fish aren't biting where you start fishing. You don't need much planning for this type of trip.

If you are going to unfamiliar waters, advanced planning can make a big difference in your success. Get a depth contour map, read articles, books and reports and see where other anglers recommend fishing. Save and file map features from fishing newspapers or magazine articles about favorite fishing places and review any that apply to the waters you will fish.

Be aware of how waters change with different seasons. If you will be fishing for anadromous fish like salmon or shad as they migrate up rivers, check fishing reports to be certain the fish are on schedule and are in the area you will plan to fish. If you are fishing for trout, they will be shallow when water is cool and in the deeper thermocline as water warms. Adjust your fishing method to account for their change in depth.

Basic Decisions

At your local lake you know certain spots produce fish early in the morning and that is where you will start to fish. If these spots slow later in the day but others improve at that time, plan to change your location to be at the new spot when you expect that to be the best. If one spot isn't producing, be prepared to try some other area. One of the advantages of trolling is it is easy to fish many different areas.

When you arrive, ask at the marina for information on where fish are being caught, how deep they are and what lures, bait or fishing methods are producing fish. Buy a map of the waterway and have someone at the marina or bait shop go over the map marking good fishing spots. Look at depth contour lines so as to locate shallow areas you should avoid. Look for good fishing spots marked on the map but be a bit suspicious of them. You will want to develop your own favorite fishing spots.

Where to Find Fish

After you launch your boat, your ability to read the water comes into play. What I have learned from people at the marina is my starting point but I only half believe what I am told. I may start trolling at the depth they recommend but I use my fish finder to refine my depth. When fish start showing up in a depth zone, I zero in on that area.

I always ask what lures have been working best, but my experience has been that the one everyone is using often isn't the best lure so I rely on old favorites to attract fish. Certain lures work for me under certain conditions. I'll probably start fishing with my favorite lures and fall back on the ones the people at the marina recommend if my favorites don't produce.

Finding fish uses a combination of insight, experience, recognizing shore features, instruments and research. Clues include looking for visible signs like surfacing fish (you often see trout breaking the surface) or diving birds chasing bait (birds are a great clue in finding bait and fish in the ocean). You may key off shore features, points, coves or surface conditions and water flow of rivers to find deep holes or fallen or submerged trees that will give fish cover. Often more subtle clues like underwater channels or structure help find fish.

Use Shore Features

Pick your area to fish then start trolling a couple hundred feet out from the shoreline. You might want to fish closer particularly if the banks are steep and the water drops off quickly but you need to stay away from anglers fishing on shore and may not be able to fish all the best spots. Trolling covers a lot of territory so you don't need to know too precisely where to fish. Points and coves are good fish producers so swing into coves as you troll. Soon you will find your favorite productive spots. These spots often change in different seasons, from year to year and even day to day, so don't be wedded to a particular fishing spot; try different areas.

Where water flows into a lake is often a good point to fish. Water brings food and feeding fish; the ones that will bite are waiting for the food.

If you have a good memory, you will soon develop a set of favorite fishing locations. To be really scientific, keep a log of your fish catches and strikes. Review your log at the end of the day and before you fish the lake or river the next time. Mark spots where you catch fish on a map of the lake or river and use that map when you fish there again.

Underwater features pinpoint areas to find fish. Sometimes trolling over a reef or along a reef is the key to finding fish. Any underwater shelf, ledge, drop-off or discontinuity signals a place fish can hide to avoid predator fish and is a good place to try.

Nothing else is as direct as a fish finder. If you keep seeing fish on your finder at a certain depth, that is where you want to fish. If you see bait, game fish will probably be right under the bait.

Finding Fish in the Ocean

In the open ocean you have no shore features to help you locate fish. Now different clues are needed. Kelp paddies in the ocean attract baitfish and may attract hundreds of game fish. Trolling past these features often catches fish. Feeding birds may signal bait is being driven to the surface by game fish attacking from below and can key location of fish.

Salmon-trollers often find a buoy is a fishing hot spot.

A trash line in the ocean marks a place where two types of water come together. It may be cold on one side and warmer on the other containing food in the seam that attracts fish.

Sometimes you see fish on your fish finder. Even seeing bait on your fish finder is a good sign as fish will be feeding on the bait. If the bait has vertical voids, game fish are probably attacking the bait and the small fish are separating to get away from the large fish. These show up as vertical veins where baitfish are absent. This is a great indicator of feeding fish so circle back and work that area before moving on.

Currents creating upwelling in the ocean provide food and draw fish. It isn't always obvious why fish are found in one location in the ocean but you can go back to that area and frequently catch fish again. Upwelling may be what attracts fish to some of these locations.

GPS or LORAN is Essential in Large Water

Navigation systems precisely pinpoint your location. For several years we have had LORAN but now Global Positioning System is more accurate, works every place in the world and is replacing LORAN. If you have LORAN and it works in your area keep using it, but if you are buying a new system, buy a GPS.

Today GPS is almost essential as a safety feature. The most important application of this navigation aid has been for safe navigation in fog or limited visibility. It is also very useful for returning to good fishing areas and helps set up good trolling patterns in the ocean.

These systems have revolutionized navigation in saltwater and in large freshwater bodies of water. Now with the price of GPS so low, their excellent accuracy and small, convenient size, they will begin to be used in many lakes and rivers.

When my fishing friend Bob Tockey first got a LORAN for his boat about 15 years ago, I fished for salmon with him and Larry Humpherys. We weren't having much success but had caught one salmon. I was piloting the boat when we caught our second salmon so I noted the LORAN coordinates. After we fished a while, I circled back toward that point. Without this navigational aid, the current and wind would take us far away from our fishing spot and we would never know if we were at or near the place where we had previously caught a fish. With LORAN we knew precisely where we were and could return to any point.

We circled back and as we got close, I kidded, "Get ready, we are almost back to the hot spot." As we got back to the coordinates, we got another hook-up. After we landed that fish we made another large circle returning to the same place and hooked fish number three. The next pass back we didn't get a fish but the one after that produced another fish. We continued making circles back to that location until we filled our six-fish limit.

The success we had catching salmon in that one hot spot was probably partly coincidence and partly returning to a school of fish. I don't ever expect to be as successful by returning to a spot as we were that day, but I know getting back to where the fish are is a key to catching fish.

Nothing is as successful as these navigational aids in returning you to a precise spot. I have tried to set a buoy then come back to it. Even drift fishing, it is amazing how far the boat drifts and how far you must run to get back to the marker. We have lost buoys in the ocean drift fishing because we drifted away from them and could never find them.

In the ocean and in large lakes, you can use LORAN or GPS to develop a trolling strategy. Plot each hit and soon you can develop a troll pattern that goes from hot spot to hot spot or tracks a school of fish as they move.

Recently I was trolling for salmon with Tom Coss. Every time we caught a fish or had a good hit, Coss would punch a way point marker that would show up on the screen of his GPS. Pretty soon he saw a line develop where we were getting hits and catching fish. By trolling back and forth along that line we were fishing where the salmon were located and I'm sure this improved our catch.

Hire a Guide

Even if your style is to always fish on your own, think about hiring a guide occasionally. You are paying for much more than a day of fishing. If you are at a new lake or river, hiring a guide for a day is an educational process. He will show you where and how to fish. Observe carefully and remember what he or she teaches you. From then on you can fish on your own with a whole new level of knowledge. Your success can improve dramatically after a single day fishing with a guide.

Your fishing success will depend largely on how well you research and plan your trip. Choose a waterway that is producing fish; learn how to fish that body of water and you will probably have a great day trolling for fish.

A dorado is on the gaff.

CHAPTER 14

Get Wired for Fish with a Black Box

Anglers know some trolling boats seem to catch fish consistently and others catch fewer fish. On a daily basis you could account for this just by luck or by being in the right place at the right time but some boats seem to always have the luck. Thoughtful observers become convinced it's not just the angler or luck, but the boat.

Studies have shown that many species of fish are attracted to electrical fields. This isn't new. Scientists have known for 100 years that positive electrical fields attract many fish. Some fish are attracted by electrical fields—others are repelled and some couldn't care less. Many of the predator fish that are our top game fish are attracted.

Nature has also provided evidence of how fish react to a strong electrical field from the electric eel. This creature, made bigger than life by movies and horror stories, does discharge a strong electrical charge that repels other fish.

Scientists in 1917 experimented with blindfolded catfish in a tank and found they were attracted to some metals put in their tank, repelled by others and had no reaction to still others. They then substituted an electrical field for the metal and found they could attract or repel these fish depending on the electrical field they imposed in the water.

Electrical Fields Attract Fish

Sharks were observed digging in sand to find flounder. They were very good at finding flounder that were buried and out of view. Researchers began experimenting to find what it was that led the shark to these fish. They suspected the small electrical field that flounder naturally produced so they buried an electrical device giving off a similar electrical field. The shark would go right to it and dig, no doubt expecting to find a flounder. The experiment was repeated over and over and shark would always go to the electrical field.

Anglers fishing for coho salmon in clear water with a proper positive charge on their downrigger observed salmon following the boat. The skipper said the fish would follow and one by one would hit a lure. He could crank up the charge and the salmon would disperse or crank it down to a lower voltage and the fish would lose interest and drift away.

This and other experiments and observations established that many fish are attracted to positive electrical fields and quantified what charge was optimum for different species.

Boats Produce an Electrical Field

Boats in the water, particularly those using downriggers, are surrounded by electrical fields. The primary source of this is the difference in electrical potential between different metals on the motor, the boat and the downriggers. Most boats have a zinc attachment to protect the metal parts from corrosion that, in conjunction with other metals, produces an electrical field around the boat.

Researchers began studying how this field may attract or repel fish. Early studies were directed toward commercial trolling boats fishing for salmon. They soon found that a positive charge of 0.6 volts on the downrigger cable would attract chinook salmon. A higher charge would repel them and a lower charge held little attraction. Different charges work best for different fish.

Researcher Malcolm Russell tells about two brothers that had identical boats except one boat consistently caught more fish. The brothers would take turns skippering the good boat, troll side by side and even interchange the equipment, but the one boat was always the best fish producer.

Commercial fishing boats are loaded with electronic gear. Some is used for communication, others for navigation like radar. It includes motors to pull lines and operate fishing gear. Wire downrigger cables suspended from trolling boats act as antennas generating their own electrical fields in the water. A charge into the water from the zinc anode—almost every outboard motor or outdrive has this item—reacting with the downrigger cable is a major contributor to this voltage difference. The field around a boat is a combination of all of these inputs.

Russell and his father evaluated the brothers' boats. The one that was the fish catcher had an ideal electrical field around the boat and downrigger cables. The one that didn't catch fish was electrically imbalanced. They concluded the electrical charge the boats were putting into the water determined how well a boat fished.

Commercial trollers have been setting up their boats with field generators (called Black Boxes) for about 30 years. Malcolm Russell and his father were pioneers in the field and the young Russell continues to make Black Boxes for commercial fishermen today. A few years ago this technology was applied to sport fishing when Scotty Downriggers produced and marketed a Black Box to use on sports fishing boats. This device, selling for about $300 was

A sacrificial zinc plate like this one is used on boats to protect other metals from corrosion. It is also the source of the beneficial field that surrounds fishing boats.

hailed as a breakthrough in sport fishing and was given the Most Innovative New Product award at the 1993 American Fishing Tackle Manufacturers show.

Modifying the Electronic Signature

Metal parts of boats that are used in saltwater are consumed by saltwater corrosion. This is an electrolytic process just like the battery in your car produces electricity. In anywhere from a few months to a few years, large parts of the prop or outdrive that are in saltwater can be pitted and eaten away.

The corrosion process is well-known and certain metals are protected while others are pitted and consumed. A galvanic table shows which metals are least subject to corrosion and which are most subject to corrosion. Gold and platinum are most resistant to this problem and materials like zinc and lead corrode quickly. Steel and aluminum, two of the most common materials in an outboard motor or outdrive are somewhere in the middle.

Zinc Anti-corrosion Devices Create Field

Zinc is important because it is used as a sacrificial metal on an outdrive. Most outdrives on outboard or an inboard/outboard motor have an inexpensive, exposed zinc part. It protects other metals by being the point of corrosion, but it is easily replaced.

A byproduct of this is that the zinc acting with other metals creates an electrical field around the boat. It makes a weak galvanic battery just like the lead acid battery in your car only the voltage is lower. When a downrigger cable is lowered in saltwater, the voltage between the stainless steel cable and the zinc is 0.8 volts.

Other factors, particularly battery current leakage from the boat's electrical system, will alter this electrical potential (another way to say voltage).

Can We Use This for Fishing?

Something in the water that will attract fish to the boat in addition to your bait, lures and flashers—that sounds great. I want every advantage I can get. Does this Black Box really attract fish? If you are trolling with downriggers, the answer is clearly yes.

In use it has gotten good reviews. Guides on British Columbia sport fishing boats claim that boats with the Black Box out-fished other boats two and three to one. Guides and anglers who use this device have high praise for the way it helps them catch fish. Tom Nelson, fishing instructor out of Seattle said, "The Black Box has consistently given me the edge over boats fishing around me with the same gear but without a Black Box."

This zinc trim tab on an outboard motor is made to protect the other metals on the boat and motor. It is replaced after it is sufficiently corroded.

Applies to Trolling with Downriggers

This only applies to trolling with downriggers and trolling lures or bait close to downrigger cables. The cable acts like an antenna and the field is created around the conductive cable.

If you are trolling with 50 or 100 feet of line behind a downrigger, your lure or bait is outside the major electrical field and this doesn't have much effect. Dick Pool has found leader lengths of 10 to 20 feet are best. If you must use longer leaders because the fish are in clear water and are spooked by the boat, the electrical attraction will have less benefit.

If you are fishing with conventional lines but don't have a downrigger in the water, you have a field around the boat but it doesn't extend to your bait or lure and won't help you catch fish. However, if you are trolling with wire line, you can create the desirable positive field. Attach the output from the Black Box to your line using an electrical clip to make the connection after your line has been spooled out to establish the desired field.

If you are mooching, the boat may have some attraction for shallow fish but not much affinity for deep fish. But this effect can be applied to mooching by attaching your mooching line to a downrigger in the water or by just putting the downrigger in the water to attract fish to the area.

Ideal Field Varies for Different Fish

If the field is too small, the fish aren't attracted as well and if the voltage is too high, it will "blow the fish off" just like a charge from an electric eel drives fish away.

Scientists have found the ideal voltage to attract chinook salmon is 0.6 and for coho it is 0.65 volts. The 0.8 natural voltage isn't too far from this level. It doesn't take much change in the electrical field around the boat to make an ideal potential. If poor grounds on the electronics modify the field just right, a boat may be naturally balanced to attract these fish. If the voltage goes in the wrong direction (to a higher level), you will drive salmon away.

For sockeye salmon the ideal potential is 0.75 volts but for sharks it is only 0.4 volts, and halibut are most attracted at a voltage of 0.45. The ideal voltage for bass is 0.75. Most trout including rainbow, brown and even lake trout have an ideal voltage of 0.65 volts. Catfish and sturgeon come to a potential of 0.5 volts. A boat that naturally has the right field for one species won't be optimum for another.

Checking Your Boat

Downriggers must be electrically isolated from the zinc for this material to protect metal parts on the boat. In a fiberglass boat, the isolation is natural. For a metal boat you need to use an insulator to electrically separate the downrigger from the boat and engine. An insulating pad where the downrigger is attached to the boat isolates the downrigger from the boat.

With your boat in the water away from other boats and electrical equipment, and the end of the downrigger cable 10 or more feet under water, check the voltage between the engine and the downrigger cable. To do this, connect the negative probe of a sensitive voltmeter to the engine block or outboard motor and touch the positive probe to the downrigger cable. In saltwater the reading should be 0.8 volts. A normal variation from 0.7 to 0.9 is okay. A similar reading made in freshwater may have more variation.

If the reading is less than 0.7 volts, the zinc protective block probably is not protecting the metal parts of the boat from corrosion. You may need to simply clean the zinc or replace it. If this isn't the cause, it is probably a poor ground in the electronics in the boat. If the voltage is higher than 0.9 volts, the boat has electrical grounding problems. Each electrical item needs to be properly grounded—the electrical connections must be clean and conductive to make a proper ground.

Check the resistance at each connection of the fuel tank to the common wire, the electrical switches and instruments to be certain they have good electrical continuity. Clean any connections that are suspect. Unless you are versed in electronics, read a more detailed book or get help in making this analysis.

Fresh water produces the same effect. If the water were absolutely pure, it would not be a conductor and would not produce this field. However, natural water found in lakes and rivers has minerals and responds much like saltwater.

Characteristics of the Black Box

The Black Box will not overcome hot spots created by leakage or high resistance in electrical connections in the boat. It will only work if all electrical connections are clean and isolated from the boat hull. The electronics in the boat must be properly grounded and the downrigger cable must not be electrically connected to the motor.

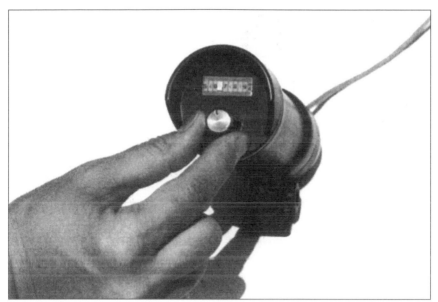

A black box like this one imparts an electric field around a boat and attracts fish.

Connect the Black Box to the downrigger cable with a metal slider provided with the unit. As many as six downrigger cables can be set up off one Black Box. The positive connection is made to the cable of the downrigger and the negative is to the ground on your boat.

Select the voltage you want from this book or from the charts supplied with the Black Box. Dial in the voltage for that fish or any minor alteration you wish to make.

The power for a Black Box is a 12 volt battery. It draws a very low power of 0.1 amp or less so it isn't a major drain on the battery.

Low Setting is Better than a High Setting

"If you aren't catching fish, reduce the voltage on the Black Box," Pool says. "If your voltage is set too high, you blast away the fish. If it is a bit low you just don't have optimum attraction." It is better to accept less than optimum, or at least experiment to see if you have better results at a slightly lower setting, than to drive fish away.

World record holder Mike Hall fishing for trout in Flaming Gorge said, "I have counted as many as 50 fish following my gear at a setting of 0.65 volts. If I run the Black Box at 0.55 to 0.60, some fish will follow but not as many. At 0.70 volts, I blow them away and none will follow."

As you can see, fish are very sensitive to too much current in the water and are repelled even by a slight increase in voltage. If you aren't having much fishing success, try turning your voltage down below the stated optimum to see if you catch more fish.

Most of the information for this chapter was supplied by Dick Pool. For further information, read *Black Box Electric Fishing Technology* by Malcolm Russell and Dick Pool.

CHAPTER 15

Refinements That Catch More Fish

Even if you apply all of the information in this book, you can still learn many more refinements that experts use to catch fish. Here are a few final thoughts on how to catch more fish when you are trolling.

After every fishing trip I could go home knowing, "I made some mistakes today." I frequently try to evaluate why I lost a fish and what I could have done differently to land this fish. I question how I could have attracted more fish. But I don't get upset—well, maybe I do when I have lost a big fish. After all fishing is a relaxation, a sport, a diversion. Being too self critical can take much of the fun from the sport. But continually striving to improve is part of the enjoyment of fishing.

Keep notes. Some people have good memories but most of us need to keep notes to remember where and how we have caught fish. These notes help plan a fishing strategy for our next trip.

Using Scents

A fish has an acute sense of smell. One way a salmon navigates back to its river or stream of origin to spawn is by distinguishing the smell of that river from all others. One stream can't smell too much different from other streams so the salmon's sense of smell must be very good to distinguish the difference. Experiments have shown these fish will react positively to very minute concentrations of a baitfish, or avoid a faint hint of a predator like a bear or a person.

You can use artificial scents to attract fish and you can take steps to mask your scent. When fishing for salmon, I crush a bait and smear oils and juices from the bait on my fingertips, on the leader, flashers or dodgers and lures to mask any residual human scent.

I don't usually use fish scents but many people do. The right ones attract fish and most anglers agree, at worst, they don't deter them. One caution is that scents are sometimes prohibited. Many rivers in Alaska, for example, forbid use of scents on lures.

Change Lures Often

If your lure isn't catching fish, make a change. I change lures about every hour unless the one I'm using is catching fish. Even when I am catching fish, I'll often change just to see what other lures are equally effective. I've built up a group of lures for trout that consistently catch fish and I use these most of the time. I also have my favorite color combinations. I usually try out a couple of new lures or new colors each day to evaluate new candidates for my list of reliable fish catchers. In the process, I find good lures but I also find some lures that seem to never catch fish.

I had one lure manufacturer tell me that lures don't have to catch fish—all they have to do is attract fishermen. So be aware that not all lures are effective. Some, at least under certain conditions, don't seem to attract many fish.

Tune Your Lures

Tune your crankbaits to run smoothly. Bend the eye on a lure to make it track straight and wobble uniformly from side to side. If it runs to the right, pick up the lure and using needlenose pliers bend its eye to the right. A small change will tune a lure to run smoothly so make a small correction. If it runs more erratically after you have bent the eye, you know you turned it the wrong way and need to bend the eye in the opposite direction.

Run Lures at Optimum Speed

Each lure or rig has an optimum trolling speed or range of speeds. Troll too slowly and you don't get enough

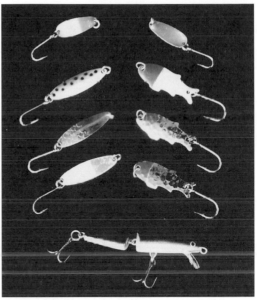

A variety of small lures and a crankbait are good lures when trolling for trout.

action; troll too fast and you kill the action or induce an unnatural action. When I fished with guide Roger Keeling at Lake Almanor, we started out with Needlefish and Triple Teazers but soon Keeling decided to try speed trolling. This is trolling at between three and four knots, about twice a normal trolling speed.

He tied a Rapala on one rig and a Speedy Shiner lure on the other. Soon we had a brown trout on a Rapala and then a rainbow trout on the Speedy Shiner. When Keeling made the change, he was careful to choose lures that would all troll well at the higher speed.

Have everyone in your boat use a lure that trolls well at a particular speed. Does this sound like you when you are fishing? Friend One decides to use a Speedy Shiner; Friend Two says he is going to use a Super Duper and you choose a Needlefish. The Speedy Shiner needs to be trolled fast; the Super Duper needs to be trolled slowly and the Needlefish is best at an intermediate speed. No way can all of these lures be fished effectively trolling from the same boat at the same time.

Crankbaits, Needlefish, Triple Teazers, Dick Nites and most other wobble lures troll well at an intermediate speed but have a wide range of acceptable speeds. These intermediate speed lures include most metal lures and crankbaits used for trout and are the basic lures I count on when I am fishing.

Other Considerations

After catching a fish or when fishing in rocks and brush, the line may become frayed and even a slightly frayed line can be a weakened line. Check your line frequently and retie. I don't use snap swivels unless they are required to avoid line twist, and I always retie when I change lures.

Many states allow anglers to use two rods under some conditions. California and Nevada sell two rod stamps that permit anglers to use a second rod on lakes. Different states may permit two rods in some situations and only one rod in others. I like the second rod. I don't believe that I catch more fish—

87

I just hook more and lose more. But the second rod lets me experiment with two lures, two depths and sometimes two fishing methods and I can learn what lure and what method works best for different conditions.

Move Weight Away From the Lure

With a conventional set up using a weight, you can only get a certain amount of separation between the bait or lure and the weight. If your leader is too long, you reel your weight to the tip of your rod and the fish is still too far away to land. Sometimes I want a lot of separation so the bait or lure is really isolated from the weight and won't spook the fish.

Here is a way to get as much separation between the weight and the bait or lure as you want and still land the fish. Use a slider (you can buy these at most tackle shops) that runs freely on the line and has a snap to attach the weight. Run the line through the slider in a normal fashion. Play out your lure and line letting it run through the slider. When you have enough separation between your lure or bait and your weight, peg the slider to the line. Make an extra loop in the line and lightly wedge the end of a round toothpick into the slider in this loop. You actually have three thicknesses of line where you wedge the toothpick to pinch the line to the inside of the slider.

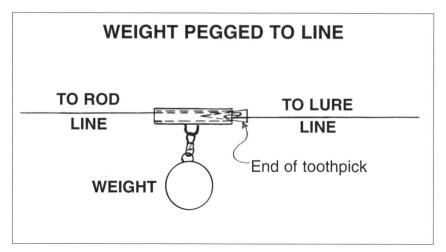

Play out your line carefully so your peg doesn't pull free prematurely. When you hook a fish, the fighting fish will pull hard enough to pop out the toothpick if it is very lightly wedged and the weight will slide to the hook, lure or swivel on the line. Experiment with this rig to get the tension of the toothpick just right. I prefer wedging the toothpick in the side of the slider nearest the weight.

Keep the loop small. The fish will get a momentary relaxation of force as the peg pulls out and the line straightens. The bend in the rod should quickly take up the slack but a small loop will minimize the slack and not risk losing fish.

When you have had a hard strike but missed the fish, the weight will probably be tripped and will slide down to the bait or lure. You need to reel in to reset the weight.

Trolling With Crankbaits

When I was growing up most artificial lures were made of wood and we called them plugs. Today most are molded plastic and are called crankbaits. Many of these have a running depth on the package or on the lure. If none is noted, you can check the size of the lip to estimate how deep they will troll. A lure with a small lip trolls about five feet deep. A larger lip may take it down to 10 to 15 feet and a really large lip can take the lure to maybe 25 or 30 feet deep. Lures like Rat-L-Traps that don't have a lip are usually shallow runners.

The depth entered on the lure or its package is usually for casting and retrieving. Here the line is fairly short and the lure doesn't run as deep as a trolled lure. The line diameter is also important—lures troll deep with a small diameter line and shallower with heavy line.

The force on a lure is all hydrodynamic. Increase the speed and its drag and diving force are both increased, but the ratio between the two stays the same. Forces on a line are also hydrodynamic and increase similarly as speed is increased. As a result, changing speed does not appreciably change the depth a lure is trolled.

The profile of the line is steep at the lure and shallow at the surface just like trolling with a weight. Understanding the contour of the line underwater offers insight into trolling with crankbaits but the graphs in this book do not apply to diving lures.

Diving Planes

Diving planes like Luhr-Jensen Pink Ladies, Dipsy Divers or Les Davis Deep Sixes will take the bait or lure to depth. These have a feature that makes them take an angle and dive but they can be tripped in some way (usually by jerking on the line) so that they will come back to the surface. These divers come in several sizes, one suitable for about every type of freshwater or saltwater fishing.

Just as it is when trolling crankbaits, the forces on divers are all hydrodynamic. As you troll faster or slower the force on the diver and the line change but they stay in balance and the diver remains at the same depth.

A Deep Six is a diving plane used to take a lure or bait to depth. A hard pull will trip the diver and it will come back to the surface.

I have used these devices but usually favor other means of getting my rig to depth. Even when they are tripped, they exert a force as a fighting fish swims laterally. I would rather play the fish without any extraneous forces. I can play the fish more carefully and have a better chance of landing a lightly hooked fish without divers on the line.

Catch-and-Release

Our fish are a limited resource. Keep only what the resource can support and you can use. If you can successfully release excess fish, do so. Don't catch too many to just give away. A neighbor lady loves fresh trout; I always try to catch a trout for her when I am catching planted fish—sometimes that is the only fish I keep. Otherwise I keep only enough for my family.

Learn the differences between planted fish and wild fish. Planted fish, the ones found mostly in urban lakes, are going to be caught or die without repro-ducing. These are the fish to keep. Wild fish must reproduce to sustain the pop-ulation and catching too many will deplete the resource. Any wild fish you release is one more fish to spawn or for someone else to have the pleasure of catching again. I don't keep any wild trout or bass.

Biologists in some states (Oregon is a notable case) clip the dorsal fin of some of their hatchery species like steelhead. They may require that you keep only hatchery fish that have the clipped fin (it looks mangled). Other times it is an indicator to you so you can keep hatchery fish and release wild fish.

Salmon are going to spawn and die. As long as plenty have escaped for spawning, keeping excess fish doesn't deplete the resource. In rivers in the lower 48 states, fishing pressure is heavy and I release most of my river-caught salmon although I keep ocean-caught fish. It may be a small distinction but when they are that close to spawning, I don't want to interrupt their destiny.

Final Thoughts
Don't make fishing too complicated by trying to incorporate everything into your trolling strategy at once. Start by asking for lure recommendations, how deep to troll and where to troll. Then follow those directions using a lure or a lure and a weight and the graphs in this book to get to depth. You can catch a lot of fish knowing only these factors.

A deckhand holds up a yellowtail for Kristan Dalton.

90

Appendix

Computing Depth

You may be asking yourself, "How did he make those calculations?" I've tried to make it easy to understand but it is a bit involved. Mathematically inclined people may want to follow this to evaluate the calculation but don't worry if this all sounds like Greek, you don't need it. Just go back to the graphs in Chapters 9 to 11 that show the depths and use them to see how deep you are trolling.

When I took partial differential equations in college, I found I could compute the path of a line through the water and the depth of a weight or lure while trolling. I needed to know forces on the weight and the line but I had some aerodynamic experience and knew I could go to textbooks to find those values. I was able to write and solve the differential equations but it was an involved analysis.

Computers were just becoming popular; personnel computers were yet to be invented so the tools to make these calculations were much cruder than today's systems. As computers became more available and more powerful, the whole method for making this computation became much easier. I only needed to write the difference equations and let the computer make billions of calculations to solve the equations. Difference equations are easier to write and much easier to solve than differential equations. A person would take weeks to make these calculations and would probably make simple errors that would invalidate the results. But a computer can do it in seconds without errors.

Start at the Weight

The procedure is to start at the weight and compute the forces acting on the weight. The line attached to the weight applies an equal and opposite force so we can calculate the force in the line and the angle the line makes coming off the weight.

With that starting point, we march up the line starting with very short lengths of line. We compute the hydrodynamic drag and lift on the short segment of line and add these to the force on the line at the weight. The force on the upper end of this segment of line is equal and opposite to the force on the lower end of the next connecting segment of line. By computing the new force and angle at the end of each segment and continuing to take many small steps along the line we walk the line all the way to the surface.

The line can be thought of as a series of straight cylinders connected at the ends. If we make those cylinders very short in the calculation, they will take on the shape of a smooth curve and the results will be accurate A computer makes many calculations fast so it is practical to make calculations for a series of short segments to get a smooth curve and an accurate result.

Forces on the Weight

The forces on the weight can be separated into vertical and horizontal forces. These forces depend on the size and weight of the sinker; water density that is the same for all depths and velocity through the water. The forces are the same whether the weight is a few inches under the water or if it is 100 feet deep.

The vertical force on the sinker is its weight in water and that acts straight down. The horizontal force is the hydrodynamic force, and since the sinker is a symmetrical sphere, it only has drag and that acts horizontally opposite the direction of travel.

If a sinker weighs two ounces, the vertical force on the sinker is two ounces down and the vertical force the line must apply to the weight is two ounces up.

If the drag force on the weight is equal to its weight, the horizontal force on the line equals the vertical force and the line starts off from the weight at a 45 degree angle. If the weight is greater than the drag force (which is usually the case), the line is steeper. The drag is dependent on the area of the weight and the square of the velocity the weight moves through the water. If the area of the weight is doubled the drag force is also doubled; if the velocity is doubled the drag force is four times greater. Velocity is very important in making these calculations.

Forces on the Line

Hydrodynamic forces on a cylinder moving through water at an angle have been measured. Here the force is separated into two parts. The first is the drag and it is the part of the force that acts opposite to the direction traveled (horizontal). The second is lift like the lift from a wing of an airplane and this acts in a vertical upward direction. The weight of the line also needs to be included, but for monofilament or Dacron line the density of the line is about equal to the density of water. Its weight in water is zero so this factor can be ignored.

We analyze the horizontal or drag force and the lift or vertical force for a line segment, add these to the vertical and horizontal forces in the line segment at the end toward the weight and come up with the force in the line segment at the end toward the boat. These forces must be balanced by the line so its angle is aligned with these forces.

The drag force on the line adds to the drag force on the weight but the lift force to the line partly counteracts the weight of the sinker.

For example, the horizontal force on an 0.5-pound (eight ounce) weight trolled 4 mph is 0.24 pounds. Of course the vertical force is 0.5 pounds and the line makes a 65 degree angler coming off the weight.

At the surface with 100 feet of 20-pound-test line at this velocity of 4 mph, the vertical force is only 0.06 pounds, the horizontal force has increased to 0.65 pounds and the line angle at the surface is 5 degrees.

As a point of interest, the line has a much larger area than the weight. The area of the spherical eight-ounce lead weight is 1.35 square inches but the area of the 100 feet of 20-pound-test line is about 22 square inches. Typical 20-pound-test line is 0.018 inches in diameter. For one-foot of line, the projected cross sectional area is 12 inches multiplied by 0.018 inches or 0.216 square inches. For 100 feet of line, the projected area of the line is 21.6 square inches, about 16 times the area of the weight.